A Journey of Friendships

Cherished bonds woven through time

By

Dr. Richard Sloan

Grosvenor House
Publishing Limited

This book is published by
Grosvenor House Publishing Ltd
Link House
140 The Broadway, Tolworth, Surrey, KT6 7HT.
www.grosvenorhousepublishing.co.uk

A CIP record for this book
is available from the British Library

ISBN 978-1-80381-868-9
eBook ISBN 978-1-80381-869-6

This book is dedicated to my best friend and love.
Kathleen Mary Sloan
1946–2015

About the author

Richard Sloan has at least twenty-two doctors in his family. He was a medical student first at University College London, and then the London Hospital Medical College. After qualifying as a doctor, he obtained a PhD for three years' work on human temperature regulation as a lecturer in Physiology. He co-invented the Zero Gradient Aural Thermometer which was manufactured and sold worldwide for a few years. He became a general practitioner in Cheltenham, Gloucestershire, and then at Tieve Tara, Airedale, Castleford from 1978 until 2005. He was a GP educator and progressed in that parallel career to become an Associate Director of Postgraduate General Practice Education for Yorkshire. He was nominated FRCGP in 2002 and awarded an MBE for Services to Medicine and Healthcare in West Yorkshire in 2011. He is a trustee of the charity Spectrum People and vice chair of a local community group, The Airedale Neighbourhood Management Board. He has lived alone for the past nine years and has no children. One of his friends describes him as a polymath. It is possibly because of this that he has developed many friendships, some of which are long standing.

Contents

Acknowledgements

My dear wife, Kath, who died in 2015, supported me to the hilt as I developed my career and hobbies that resulted in our both having many friends and acquaintances. I learned such a lot from her, and this has contributed to the thoughts explored for, and the approach I had towards writing this book.

I am grateful to my school in Wakefield (Queen Elizabeth Grammar School), where I not only made lifelong friends, but also sewed the seed of continuous learning. This seed was nurtured by my university education, and then by my becoming a teacher and educationalist for general practitioners in Yorkshire. Education and friends are the antidotes to loneliness.

My thanks to Grosvenor House Publishing Ltd. for the clear advice for my self-publishing this book. I was very pleased when I used them for my last book, *Tieve Tara*. I learned such a lot from that experience.

Thank you once again to Hannah Jones for undertaking the proofreading. (hannahjones@theremedyoferrors.com)

Royalties and any other profits from this book will be donated to CAFOD (the Catholic Agency for Overseas Development) and the charity Children of Peace.

Front cover - The Goodenough children with Richard Sloan in the middle

Preface

I have published two previous books, *Tieve Tara* and *The English Doctor*, each of which had a strong theme throughout. In 2021, I decided to write a third book, with no theme whatsoever. It would be a collection of essays and reflections about diverse areas of my thoughts and experiences. I would be free to write about anything whatsoever. This freedom would be in addition to the freedom experienced by self-publishing.

When my friend, Professor Stephen Shalet visited me, I joked that I could even write a chapter on professors! We laughed. A week later, I was writing a chapter on professors. I know several professors. Some of them are my friends.

The chapters published in this book are not in the order they were written. When I got to the chapter on social class, I realised that the theme throughout was friendship. I wrote the chapter on friendship last.

One problem I come across is that when I tell someone that the book is about friendship, I am often asked, "Am I in it?" He or she usually is. Of course, I worry that I will upset someone by forgetting to give them a mention in the book. I seriously regretted not mentioning Norman Batty in the book *Tieve Tara*. I have made amends in this book. I apologise if there is a friendship omission in this book.

There have been many articles and books published about friendship. One of the earliest was by the philosopher Aristotle (384 to 322 BC). Here are a couple of quotes from his work:

> "To be friends ... [the parties] must feel goodwill for each other, that is, wish each other good, and be aware of each other's goodwill."

"Wishing to be friends is quick work, but friendship is a slow ripening fruit."

Emily Katz, Assistant Professor of Ancient Greek Philosophy, Michigan State University, paraphrased Aristotle:

"Friends who are ... parted are not actively friendly yet have the disposition to be so. For separation does not destroy friendship absolutely, though it prevents its active exercise. If, however, the absence be prolonged, it seems to cause the friendly feeling itself to be forgotten."

Alexander Hurst wrote (*The Guardian*, December 2023) an article discussing the difference between male, female, and mixed sex friendships: "too often, male, friendships, end up, being emotionally stunted, stuck in banter, alone, with too much left unacknowledged, such as how much we really mean to each other".

After the loss of a partner, it is rare to see two men going on holiday together, compared with two women. Single men are the lonelier group than single women. Are mixed sex friendships always platonic? Can a dog be a friend? What is a Facebook friend? Do friendships always have to be face-to-face? Is Aristotle right that friendships must be two-way. Many more questions have come to me by writing this book, and I hope the book stimulates questions for those who read it.

This book is not an academic description of friendship. It is a collection of my thoughts and experiences that have the thread of friendship throughout in my opinion. The reader might find other threads that I have not mentioned.

CHAPTER 1

Bridging the divide: Friendships across class boundaries

This chapter is about my thoughts about social class. I started writing it on 20 May 2022. You will see why the date of writing this introduction is important as you read on.

I will reflect as honestly as I can how I see myself in the social class system of the United Kingdom. I start from a point where I believe I am middle class brought up by middle-class parents. It will be interesting to see if this opinion is as strong or stronger at the end of this chapter. I am worried that I might upset friends or relations by making negative comments about the classes. I feel that I, like many general practitioners, had long-standing professional relationships with people of social classes other than my own. In addition, I had a 37-year very happy marriage to Kath, my late wife, who was brought up by working-class parents.

On the evening of 19 May 2022, I attended a Mass at Saint Joseph's Catholic Church, Castleford, as part of the launch of a local Union of Catholic Mothers. It was my late wife's church, and I was invited by Kathryn Waugh, a friend of Kath. When I walked into the church, I noticed that Yvonne Crewe was there with her sister. I sat behind her. Yvonne was the Wakefield Metropolitan District Councillor of our Airedale and Ferry Fryston ward for sixteen years. I first met her in about 2008 and asked her advice about my doing some voluntary work. She suggested I join her on a body called the Airedale Neighbourhood Management Board.

Her husband, Phil, had died three weeks prior to the Mass after a short illness. I had been to her house and left a card and some sweets. I did not go in. I wrote a poem on the card to Yvonne. This is the poem:

Do not stand at my grave and weep.
I am not there I do not sleep.
I am a thousand winds that blow.
I am the diamond glints on snow.
I am the sunlight on ripened grain.
I am the gentle autumn rain.
When you awaken in the morning's hush
I am the swift uplifting rush
Of quiet birds in circled flight.
I am the soft stars that shine at night.
Do not stand by my grave and cry.
I am not there I did not die.
Mary Elizabeth Frye

Yvonne and Phil worked hard, very often together, for the Labour Party, our community, and the Wakefield district. They were a very kind couple.

After the Mass we retired to another room and had a cup of tea and some snacks. It was then I had the loveliest long conversation with Yvonne. We talked about Phil, of course. We compared our backgrounds. Yvonne described herself as working class and told me about her childhood and background in the Labour Party, some of which I already knew. I responded by saying "I am thoroughly middle class." She replied, "No. You are one of us." That was very nice thing to say to me and I felt it was not just Yvonne being polite. She really meant it. This was a very significant thing for me. When I got home, I felt quite emotional. You can maybe see why I started writing this chapter the very next morning.

The next evening Yvonne was taken ill at our constituency Labour Party meeting. She had visual symptoms and was rushed to Pinderfields Hospital, Wakefield. A brain haemorrhage was diagnosed. We were told that it was unlikely she would survive.

Phil's funeral went ahead on the morning of 31 May at the Holy Cross church in Airedale. There was someone from the family with

Cllr. Kathryn Scott and they sat with Yvonne as she was dying. I got to the church very early because I knew it would be packed. When I looked at the order of service it included the poem. I was amazed. Their son, Jonathan, later confirmed to me that Yvonne had requested the poem to be read by the Rev. Tracy Ibbotson, the C of E parish priest. (Phil was not a Catholic.) There was a beautiful eulogy delivered by Yvette Cooper, our MP. She and her husband, Ed Balls, were friends of the Crewe family. Yvonne told me after the Mass mentioned above, of the many acts of kindness and friendship from them over the years. She told me that during Phil's final illness Yvette and Ed turned up with fish and chips and Ed did the washing up.

On the evening of Phil's funeral, I came back home from a choir rehearsal. I opened my emails and there was one from Mike Dixon, chair of the Airedale Neighbourhood Management Board. He informed me that Yvonne had died that afternoon. The afternoon of her husband's funeral.

Yvonne and me, 2019. Photo – Cllr. David Jones

A few days later, I was overwhelmed and honoured that their son, Jonathan, asked me to read Psalm 23 and another reading from the Bible at his mother's funeral. The main reading was by Kathryn Waugh. The Mass took place in Saint Joseph's Church, Castleford, where I had last spoken to Yvonne and where the funeral of my wife Kath took place in 2015. It was a packed church and, again, Yvette gave a wonderful eulogy during which she shed a tear.

In the congregation there were people from the Castleford rugby league club (the Tigers), from Unite, the union of Yvonne, people from the political world as well as locals.

May Yvonne and Phil rest in peace.

My mother, Gerda, was brought up in a very privileged family in Berlin. Her father was a wealthy businessman/lawyer and lived in a magnificent house in the centre of Berlin. Below is a photograph of one of the downstairs rooms.

Drawing room in Berlin house, early 1930s

My mother and her two brothers had an English governess called Miss Henderson. The siblings could speak English better than German as they were growing up. My mother qualified as a doctor just before she had to get out of Berlin because of her Jewish background. She married my father, a general practitioner working in Airedale, Castleford. She became not only his married partner but also his GP medical partner. The bulk of her parents' furniture and artworks from the German house was destroyed in the Second World War. I have a dream of finding some priceless painting that was stolen by the Nazis! My mother was keen on riding and owned a horse. Her parents owned a racehorse called Battlecruiser. She was a young woman in the 1920s. I am sure she had a whale of a time in Berlin when she was a late teenager and beyond. So what class was my mother? I would label her as German old money upper class. Her uncle Ernst became a professor of biochemistry at Cambridge University after he left Germany. Her cousin Gerhard was a professor of political science at Québec University and an expert on Outer Mongolia. His father bought an island north of Germany at one point. My mother told me that I should think of my grandfather as the German equivalent of Lord Arnold Goodman, who was a leading London lawyer and advisor to Harold Wilson.

My father was a doctor and his father a headmaster of a junior school in Northern Ireland.

Did my mother become middle class when she married my father and worked in Castleford? I think so. She was brought up upper class and then lived a middle-class life after she married my father. They lived in the house where I live now. This house is a five-bedroomed property with the surgery semi-detached. It has a large double garage and a relatively large garden and is situated with six other houses on a private driveway. When I was a child, we had a gardener, housekeeper and a man who washed the cars. My parents owned another house about 1 ½ miles away where Mr. and Mrs. Firth lived rent and rates free. Mr. Firth was employed by my father to make a valiant attempt to collect the money owed for medical services provided before the NHS. I use the word 'valiant' because everyone was so poor in the late twenties and the thirties. They could not afford to pay and were often let off owing anything. After the NHS was founded, after Mr. Firth had died, Mrs. Firth took messages and visit requests. In the early 1960s my parents bought a third house to accommodate a new partner until he settled down and bought a property.

I regard myself as a part-time only child. I was an only child of my mother. My father had three children from his first marriage. My half-brother and two half-sisters showed nothing but kindness and love towards me the whole of their lives. Indeed, my half-brother,

Frank, used to tell me off if I called him a half-brother. He banned my using the word "half". Frank lived with us for a short time, and he was with us on one summer holiday in Bavaria. He joined the merchant navy and was on very long voyages at first. He often spent some of his leave with us and showered me with presents.

There was no class barrier created between my family and the working-class people who lived in council houses virtually next door. The Ward family were an example of how our classes integrated as friends.

From left to right – top, my mother, Muriel Ward, Fred Ward
Then Harold Ward, me, George Goodenough, Frank Ward,
Elizabeth then Michael Dunn on his mother, Geraldine Dunn's knee

Geraldine was my half-sister. Frank Ward, and one of his neighbours, Norman Wilson, were my best friends for years. I still see Frank occasionally and I am sure we regard one another as old friends. This integration when I was a child set me up for a life of friendly relationships and friendships regardless of class, creed, or race.

One of my heroes over the past few years has been Sir Michael Marmot. He is an expert on health inequalities. I was fortunate to hear him at a lunchtime lecture in January 2016 at my alma mater, University College London. I took this photograph of him.

Sir Michael Marmot, 19 Jan 2016

He chaired an independent of government committee which undertook a strategic review of health inequalities in England post-2010. The report was entitled "Fair Society, Healthy Lives" and is known as the Marmot Review. Here are some quotes from that review:

"What a child achieves during early years puts down a foundation for the whole of their lives."

(Early years includes preschool and from 0 to 3)

"Educational outcomes are affected by income, parental education, parental support and parent/child relationships."

"The social position of parents accounts for a large proportion of the difference in education attainment between higher and lower achievements."

Our house was one of love, happiness and learning for me in my very early years. The environment provided by my parents both in my early and later life at home was such that I would have to rebel and work very hard to not get on in life. I think I was spoiled by my parents, and it was great! They were quietly keen on my education which was a journey towards university education. I never felt pressurised. My early years (before I went to school, mentioned above) were filled with playing with toys, helping me to read and write at home, bedtime stories, wonderful holidays, happy Christmases, parties, lots of friends.

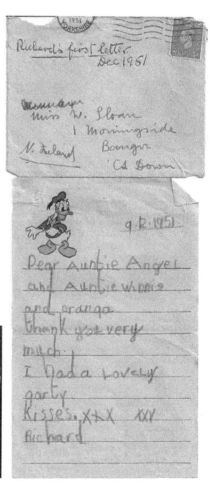

| Playing my first gramophone with my mother | First letter written aged 6 (just). (Envelope written by mother) |

Me and my trumpet

I went to the Airedale Primary Mixed School, Castleford, an infants' school. It was about a mile away from our house. My mother took me there and back by car. Not many of my neighbours were taken to school by car in those days. When I drive past now, as the school is finishing for the day, the traffic jams are huge. There have been comments that some of the parents are lazy and should be walking their children to school to prevent obesity.

I was in Mrs. Abbott's class.

Infants' school report

I am not sure how old I was when I moved from the Airedale school to the fee-paying junior school of Queen Elizabeth Grammar School, Wakefield (QEGS). The report was from my last year in the infants. One of my best friends now was in that class with me. That friend, Rosslynne Wheeldon, had to stay on for an extra year because the girls' equivalent school to QEGS, Wakefield Girls' High School, did not accept pupils until they were older. I write more about Rosslynne in Chapter 8. Rosslynne's parents owned a successful grocers' shop attached to a large house and garden. Most children at that school were from working-class backgrounds but not exclusively. My parents encouraged me to make friends with working-class boys and girls (boys mainly) both from school and from the neighbouring council houses. This has been a huge influence on my being very comfortable, all my adult life, with both working-class and middle-class people. The only friendship that persisted from those days in the infant school was the one with Rosslynne. However, when I came back to work in Airedale in 1978, a significant number of my childhood friends became patients. There is still that bond of friendship between us.

I was at QEGS junior school for three or four years and was in my eleventh year when I moved to the senior school.

QEGS was a direct grant grammar school. These were selective secondary schools and one had to pass the eleven-plus as well as an entrance examination to be admitted to the senior school. There was a relatively small fee my parents paid. Like public (private) schools, it was a member of the Headmasters' Conference. The school had a few boarding pupils. It became a fully private school in about 1975. These schools were middle-class institutions (Wikipedia). I am sure it gave us a much better education than local grammar schools and a big advantage for getting into elite universities such as Oxford and Cambridge. My headmaster, Ernest Baggaley, was the first headmaster since the foundation of the school in 1591 not to go to Oxford or Cambridge! He obtained a Geography degree at London University. The main sport at the school was rugby union, which I hated, but I was allowed to play tennis and golf when I got to the sixth form. No football! No rugby league!

Mr. Baggaley wanted as many sixth-formers as possible to apply for a place at an Oxbridge university. This would mean staying on for a third year at school. Three of us applied to London medical schools behind his back. I was offered a place to start my medical studies at University College London (UCL). My first choice was the London Hospital Medical College, but I was turned down at interview. In the middle of my interview for UCL, the interviewer, Dr. (later Professor) Prakash Datta (see Chapter 2), suddenly exclaimed something like: "What the hell is this?" as he was looking at my application form. I thought I had written something terribly wrong. However, he told me that his surprise was because he knew my headmaster, Mr. Baggaley. I think he may have been taught by him. That is the only thing I remember about that interview, and I have a feeling it is the main reason I was accepted.

Whilst at UCL, I did an extension of my medical studies to undertake a BSc in Anatomy. The head of department was the world-famous Professor J. Z. Young. The BSc was a research degree and there were twelve of us working closely with JZ, as he was known. After that course the twelve of us would move onto clinical studies at the University College Hospital (UCH). However, JZ told us that UCH was like a "boring vicarage". (I don't think it was at all.) He said he had contacts such that he could get any of the BSc students into any clinical medical school in the country. One of us went to Oxford and I was accepted by the London Hospital Medical College after a very short interview.

Why do I mention these interviews? It is because progress in a career or life in general is often because of whom you know rather than what you know. I knew Mr. Baggaley and J. Z. Young.

Most of my close school friends ended up in good professional jobs. An actuary, doctors, a professor, etc. My middle-class upbringing, therefore, gave me great advantages from my school that fed into a good career. It was often the case that one or both parents of my friends at school had professional or senior management jobs. In the 1950s and early 1960s it was relatively rare for a mother to have such a job. Examples of jobs of the fathers of some my closest secondary school friends are (in brackets, the Christian names of my friends): borough water engineer (Peter), coal mine manager (Paul), teacher and vicar (Kevin), headmaster (Colin).

Just before I started university, my parents bought me a car, a Hillman Imp. During my six years at medical school, they bought me two more cars, both Triumph Spitfires. They were all brand new. A Triumph Spitfire in those days cost the equivalent of about £9000 in today's money. My parents' double garage at home was large enough such that I could park my car between theirs.

The garage, 2022

Grants to universities were means-tested, so my parents topped up the £50 a term minimum grant for me to the level of other students' grants. They occasionally gave me some extra. I never had to have a holiday job. I never had a student loan. I was never expected to pay any money back my parents. How fortunate is that compared to today and the student loans situation?

When I started at UCL, I felt there was a significant number of fellow students much posher than I. Certainly, there were some posh accents. I assumed they were from a higher class than I. There were several with double-barrelled names. At the same time, there was a small minority of the year from working-class backgrounds. In the first eighteen months of being a student I lost weight and was quite anxious about the learning. I assumed the posh accents and the confidence of these students meant they were academically better than I. When I looked at the first exam results of those with double-barrelled surnames, I had a confidence boost. I got better marks than them. I am reminded of Harry Enfield's Tim Nice-But-Dim character.

I undertook my clinical medical studies at the London Hospital Medical College. After three years I qualified as a doctor and then undertook a year of house officer jobs, first at Mile End Hospital (part of The London and just down the road) and then back at The London working in casualty (known as The Receiving Room). After I registered as a doctor, I became a lecturer in physiology at the college. This was a teaching and research post, which I held for three years. I was therefore working in jobs related to the London Hospital Medical College for seven years.

The culture and my experience at the London Hospital was, I realise now, very different from that of University College London. UCL has a fantastic reputation for high-quality research. Researchers there have won one to four Nobel Prizes for science each decade from 1900 until now. While I was there, our Physiology professor, Andrew Huxley, won the Nobel Prize for Medicine, and I am proud that I was in his tutorial class for a term. The lectures at UCL were open to all students and there were lots of extracurricular groups one could join. At one point I had a go at indoor target shooting. There were also debates and I remember one where one of the debaters was David Frost. UCL was a left-wing organisation and sometimes called "the Godless University" compared with King's College London, which was a Christian organisation. The university was situated next door to the University of London Union and there were events going on there that one could attend. The relationship between teachers and students was a friendly one, which contrasted with some of the medical consultants who taught us later. The Professor of Anatomy, J. Z. Young, mentioned above, was at one time the Vice-President of the Royal Society, the most prodigious scientific organisation in the UK. He gave one of the Reith Lectures for the BBC in the early 1950s. There was a friendly and mutual respect between him and his students. He taught me a lot about mutual respect between people whatever their skills, intelligence, knowledge, seniority, or class.

The London Hospital and its college were much smaller than UCL. I cannot remember any fellow student at The London who came from a working-class background. My friend, Colin Teasdale, like me, undertook the extra eighteen months to complete a BSc in Anatomy at The London. He told me there was a PhD student in that department whose father was a dustbin man, aka refuse collector. This background was regarded as remarkable.

As well as searching the internet, I have used two reference books for this chapter:

"The Class Ceiling. Why it pays to be privileged." Friedman and Laurison. Bristol University Press. 2019. (1). This is an in-depth book discussing a research study which includes many interviews of people from diverse backgrounds and employed in differing working environments.

And "Social class in the 21st Century". Mike Savage et al. Pelican Books. 2015. (2)

I will use the numbers in brackets as reference labels. I would like to consider some evidence about privilege and elitism.

From (1):

"…professions of medicine, law architecture and journalism contain particularly high concentration of people from privileged backgrounds. In contrast, technical professions such as engineering and IT contain a higher than average (among these top jobs) percentage of the upwardly socially mobile."

"Microclass reproduction is the tendency of children to follow directly in their parents' occupational footsteps."

"People with parents who are doctors are a somewhat staggering 24 times more likely to be doctors than those whose parents did any other type of work."

From (2):

Findings from the BBC's Great British Class Survey were published in 2013. It was the largest survey of social class ever conducted in Britain. Part of this was the development of a class calculator which is on the internet today (2022). I answered the questions to the best of my ability. The first attempt resulted in my being labelled "technical". I thought that was not correct. I then completed the questions more carefully, possibly subconsciously swinging the answers towards a class more to my liking. Then I was labelled as in "the elite", which I don't necessarily agree with or possibly don't like. Or am I rather angling to be labelled middle class? Do readers who know me think I am middle class or what? After I completed this chapter, I knew I am middle class. I am probably thought of as letting the side down by having working-class friends.

I became a doctor. Both my parents were doctors. On my father's side of the family there were well over twenty doctors. I am an example of the microclass reproduction mentioned above.

My mother read widely and was a cultured woman. She took me and my father to the ballet at the Leeds Grand Theatre. I remember going to a performance of Handel's Messiah by the Castleford Choral Union. My father was a patron of that choir. I was about 10 years old and was rather bored until the conductor, Elsie Travis, accidentally threw her baton over her left shoulder, and it landed in the audience. My mother's father knew the famous German tenor, Richard Tauber. He performed at the Leeds Grand Theatre on one occasion, and my father was thrilled when my mother took him backstage to meet Tauber. My mother exposed me to cultural experiences.

My school in Wakefield introduced us to singing as well as lessons on classical music. The lessons were taken by the organist at Wakefield Cathedral, Dr. P. G. Saunders. He was the organist from 1945 to 1970. He explained the structure of pieces of classical music slowly and in detail. He played these on a gramophone. For example, he taught us the differences between the four movements of a symphony. The first symphony he played to us was Beethoven's Eighth. I love it to this day. The other piece of music I remember and love now is Schubert's Trout Quintet. I got into popular music to an extent in the sixties when I was at university. One could not help liking the Beatles, the Rolling Stones and, later, Queen. I now have a broad taste in music, which includes fado, Spanish tango, Gilbert and Sullivan, Janis Joplin, George Formby, Mozart, and many other classical composers. A friend, Pam Heseltine, tipped me off that one could buy the complete works of Mozart on CDs for a reasonable price. I think there are over 100 discs. I did buy them.

Complete works of Mozart on CDs

The sixth form in my school had an amazing and possibly unique curriculum where one third of the lessons were on art, music, German for scientists, etc. The other two thirds were devoted to the A-level subjects required for university entrance. However, we were encouraged to take a general studies A-level as well as the three other A-levels. I did very well in general studies when it was the mock exam but mucked up the real thing and only got a D. When it came to applying for a university place, the senior English master prepared a reading list for the holiday periods. In those days, in the early 1960s, one was expected to discuss what one had read out of school at the interview. There was a broad, cultural education going on throughout my time in the senior school.

17

When I got to university, I went to classical concerts in the Festival and Albert Halls. I usually went with friends. Gerda and Henry Tintner were both GPs in Roehampton and were long-standing close friends of my parents. They were very generous and sometimes bought two tickets for a Sunday concert at the Albert Hall. One ticket was for me and the other for their au pair girl. I particularly enjoyed those concerts! I also went to theatre productions. I went with friends, including Grahame Smith, to a Harold Pinter play. I found it difficult. However, as with most of these cultural experiences of my youth, age matured my approach to things that were difficult. I eventually admired Harold Pinter and Chekhov greatly. I persist in trying to like difficult cultural experiences. This has partly resulted in my having a very broad taste in the arts. I have an interest in all these things, but not necessarily a great knowledge.

So, what are my general conclusions about all this? Education is the crux. A middle-class background with cultured and relatively wealthy parents were catalysts to my fulfilled life. I cannot emphasise enough what value it was to my life, having a university education. It is serving me well now when I live alone.

"A large body of epidemiologic data show that diet quality follows a socio-economic gradient. Whereas higher quality diets are associated with greater affluence, energy-dense diets that are nutrient-poor are preferentially consumed by people of lower socio-economic income and of more limited economic means."

Does social class predict diet quality? Nicole Darmon, Adam Drewnowski.

The American Journal of Clinical Nutrition, Volume 87, Issue 5, May 2008, Pages 1107–1117.

I have discussed diet and obesity with my working-class patients when I was a general practitioner. I have observed patients preparing meals in their homes. I have heard about the diet situation of many of the children in this deprived area of Airedale, Castleford, since I have been a member of a community group for the past fifteen years.

They are arriving at school hungry. The Airedale food bank is overwhelmed. Volunteers are providing lunch for children in the school holidays. What a terrible situation.

I mainly discussed diet with diabetics and obese patients, and really did not know much about the general diet of my patients. Often, in patients' homes, there was bacon, gently frying in the kitchen. I rarely saw a bowl of fruit. Lots of bread. Since my childhood, there were always about four or five fish and chip shops in Airedale, which has a population of about 16,000. As time went on, the fish and chip shops survived, and more and more takeaways opened. Here they are:

Sizzlers Vs Pronto Pizza
Orient Delight
I Love Paradise Pizza Ltd.
Krunchy Chicken
Triangle Café
Taj Mahal
Golden Sun
The Kitchen
Cas Vegas

There are four fish and chip shops.

I rarely use a fish and chip shop now. In the 1980s I used one where I knew I would get a huge portion of chips served by a patient. I could never finish them. The last time I went to a fish and chip shop in Airedale was before the pandemic started. I had never seen such a huge portion of chips. I was chatting to the server and asked what time they closed. It was just a bit of small talk. She replied "Why? Are you coming back for a second helping?"

I mention these portions because it is generally accepted that obesity is more significant in lower classes compared with the privileged classes. I have observed that in some pubs in the area where I live, very large portions are served, particularly the main course. I found that my patients did not take much notice of dietary advice from the

NHS, and I nearly gave up on it. It is usual to start listening to dietary advice only after suffering one of the medical consequences of obesity rather than trying to prevent these. On the other hand, I have two middle-class friends who seem to totally ignore the dietary advice one should follow with insulin-dependent diabetes.

Education has a huge role to play in the approach of people to dietary intake. My mother taught me to try to like a large variety of different foods, and I believed this worked as I can honestly say it is difficult for me to think of anything now I could not eat. If initially I am not keen on something I try it again and, often, grow to like it. A bit like the difficult art and music I mentioned above.

It is worth my pointing out that I am overweight and have been so almost continuously since I was a child. I was only slim during one period of my life, and that was after I started as a medical student. My father died around about that time. Now, I drink rather too much wine in the evenings! Merlot.

I have been married twice. The first time was to Felicity for seven years. She was from a middle-class background. The second time was to Kathleen for thirty-six years (Kath died after a short illness in February 2015). She was from a working-class background. So, there is another illustration of parental class and its influence on their children that I have personally experienced at close quarters.

Felicity's father, Bill, was the deputy water engineer for Liverpool, a senior position. Felicity's parents lived in a nice area of Liverpool and a relatively large house. Her father was a freemason and her mother, Pat, a Soroptimist. When I first met Pat, I thought she said she was a chiropodist! I had never heard of a Soroptimist at that time.

Kath's father, Charlie, was a railway engine driver and an active trades unionist. Kath's parents lived in a small house in the village of Woodford Halse in Northamptonshire. I met her father when we went out as students. He died in the period between then and when Kath and I met again in the second half of the 1970s. Her mother,

Hilda, who was a secretary, was also involved with the union. Hilda was very keen on Kath having a university education, which did not go down well with some people in her village. Going to university was regarded by some working-class people as "la di da" and a waste of time when one could be earning.

Because of the difference in the length of those two marriages, it is difficult to make comparisons. The first wedding was formal, with the groom, best man and more men wearing top hat and tails. By the way, I am the nineth cousin twice removed of Fred Astaire!

"I'm putting on my top hat,
Tying up my white tie,
Brushing off my tails."
Written by Irving Berlin for the 1935 film "Top Hat" and performed by Cousin Fred.

Me (right) and my best man (Robin Harrod) at Felicity's and my wedding

The reception was at Liverpool Airport.

The second wedding was at Banbury Registry Office, followed by a reception at Whately Hall in Banbury.

Kath (right) and I at our wedding, with her maid of honour,
Gill Kavanagh

Felicity qualified as a doctor at Saint Mary's Hospital in London. She became a general practitioner in Cheltenham. She remarried and had two children. We contact one another occasionally. Her sister, Penny, also lives in Cheltenham. We exchange Christmas cards and I have visited them once not so many years ago. It was lovely to meet her and her husband, Andrew, once again.

Kath obtained a degree in Spanish and Portuguese at King's College London. She was the lady vice-president of King's. This was an elected post, and the main work was organising and contributing to social events. She worked for several years in London in the surveying world. Her last job in London was in a small company, which was, in essence, an employment agency for surveyors.

After the breakdown of the first marriage, Felicity remained in Cheltenham. Kath and I moved up to Airedale, Castleford, and set up the general practice there. Kath and I were not blessed with children, and she had two main jobs. One was the deputy manager of Nostell Priory Enterprises, which was owned by Rowland Denys Guy Winn, 4th Baron Oswald. Nostell Priory is a stately home. It is now owned and managed by the National Trust. The objectives of the enterprises company involved putting on huge events, weddings, and much more. Lord St. Oswald died in 1984 and Kath returned to our medical practice as Practice Manager. Kath really got on with him and could not work there with anyone else as her employer.

Kath took part in what I regarded as serious academic studies. One was a University of Leeds course on renaissance art. We owned a house in Umbria which we visited regularly. There was a written examination at the end. Another was a two-year part-time course run by the Wine and Spirits Education Trust. She obtained a level three advanced certificate in Wines and Spirits, with Distinction. I did not realise until now that this was a qualification not only for wine enthusiasts but also for professionals working in the wine industry. We bought two wine coolers, one for white wine and one for red. Kath stocked them with some great bottles. She was very keen on classical music. We attended operas and concerts both at home and abroad. Kath was a cultured and well educated, well-read woman. However, she had a bit of a chip on her shoulder about her working-class background, which I thought was ridiculous. It was easy for me to think that. I did not have any worries about my class. Some of the middle-class people we met seemed to us to be showing off their wealth and possessions. It did not bother them or me, but it bothered her. Some middle-class people who were brought up working class are the worst at showing off. This group also have a habit of being rude to waiters and waitresses. One can see part of the character of a person by observing how he or she behaves with those serving at table.

My conclusion is that university education and marriage are great levellers. Friends of mine who have been to university have a thirst for further learning and this can be formal or informal, at an educational institution or at home. It is not relevant whether members of this group have been brought up in a working-class family or not. The further learning, I have observed, includes languages, learning a musical instrument, painting, woodwork, Open University courses after retirement, singing in a choir, etc. I did not observe many of my patients in the deprived area where I worked undertaking such activities as their lives progressed. They had other matters on their minds, such as poverty, looking after their children, unemployment, social misbehaviour as well as drug and alcohol misuse. Lifelong education might be judged by them as a luxury.

Two of my closest friends, Kath Overton and her husband, Alan, were brought up working class in the same village as my Kath. They undertook lots of courses and joined groups outside their work. Alan has self-published a couple of books. There is a significant number like them in the UK. However, this freedom was facilitated by their work ethic and being able to afford time to devote to these activities, which was easier after the children left home. We four discussed social class often. We joked about the different experiences between me and the three of them in our youth. For a joke, I once bought Kath Overton a book for Christmas: *A Plain Cookery Book for the Working Classes*.

I want you to know about my invention of the phrase "rich pigs' worries". Many years ago, I worked as a GP tutor for Pontefract and Castleford GPs. The job was based in the postgraduate centre at Pontefract Hospital. The commitment was two half-days a week. I worked very closely with Dr. Michael Peake, a respiratory medicine consultant, responsible for the postgraduate education at the hospital. One Friday, he came rushing into the postgraduate centre office in a bit of a state. He said he was anxious. He had to go to London to buy a new cover for his swimming pool. That was when I invented the phrase "rich pigs' worries". If one has insight and can diagnose when one is experiencing a rich pigs' worry, one can kick oneself and realise how lucky one is. The inappropriate stress then disappears.

After all my reflection about my thoughts on social class, was Yvonne right when she said to me "You are one of us"? Why did I get so emotional when she said that? She said that in our conversation about our social class status that I described at the start of this chapter. She knew I empathised with the working-class people of Airedale, and she had observed me developing friendly relationships and friendships with working-class people. She knew of the mutual respect I had with working-class people. She knew I was not a snob or intentional show-off. She really meant she accepted me as a fellow member of the community. That is a great compliment for the son of immigrants. My parents and others taught me these behaviours and qualities and for that I am so grateful.

I have been, am and will remain thoroughly middle class.

Said by George Osborne, Conservative Conference, 2012

CHAPTER 2

Professors

I joked to one of my friends, who is a professor, that because of the freedom of self-publishing, I might write a chapter on professors. I thought no more about that joke for quite a while and then decided I really could write such a chapter. When I mentioned this to a second professor, who is also a friend, and who is writing a history book, he replied that if I was not nice about him, there would be a publishing war! These two friends have been great motivators as regards my writing and they are David and Steve (see below).

Professors are usually in a professional role with respect to students. However, if one is a member of a small class or group with a professor, then a closer and more friendly relationship might develop. I had a close working relationship with Bill Keatinge when he was my PhD supervisor. I had a close working relationship when I was in a small group undertaking a BSc in Anatomy with Professor J. Z. Young. I am fortunate that I have two long-standing friends who became professors and I know other professors I regard as friends. This chapter might demonstrate that professors are human and approach life just like I do and many of the readers of this book.

Professor is the most senior academic staff grade. Generally, professors in universities have PhDs, but that is not mandatory. There are several academic grades less senior than a professor: associate professor, senior lecturer, and lecturer. There are also research assistants – senior, postdoctoral, etc. Some universities have the staff grade of "reader". Readers are at a similar level as associate professors and usually become professors. Some universities, such as Leeds, have dispensed with the reader grade which was common in my day.

Emeritus professor is an honorary title given to a distinguished academic professor who has retired. Some UK universities award all retiring professors this title. Other universities award the title only to those who have made distinguished contributions to their subject.

A visiting professor will usually be from another university. The attachment can be for a couple of months or longer. Sometimes the university expects the visiting professor to have equivalent national or international experience and standing as a UK professor.

An honorary professor might be appointed with an objective of strengthening links with industry, the arts, etc. The appointment might also be because of a significant research or teaching contribution. The person should be worthy of a chair and often is eminent in their field. My impression is that honorary professor appointments might be more common in the USA. Examples of professors in American universities are Placido Domingo, John Cleese, Kevin Spacey and Jimmy Carter. Certainly, the use of the title of professor is allowed for associate and assistant professors in the USA. One must be a "full" professor to use the title in the UK.

One reason I decided to write this chapter is that I realised I had come across a significant number of professors in my working and retired life. I will quote some of their achievements. I have researched the internet for these quotes.

1. Professors I know now

David Waddington

David Waddington

"Since joining Sheffield Hallam University (then Sheffield City Polytechnic) as a postdoctoral research associate in March 1983, I have been involved in two principal areas of research: the policing of public disorder; and the social implications both of the 1984-85 miners' strike, and the pit closure programme occurring in its wake. I became Head of the CCRC in February 2008 and was Chair of our College Research Ethics Committee from July 2007 to September 2013." https://www.shu.ac.uk/about-us/our-people/staff-profiles/ david-waddington Accessed 22 12 21. CCRC = Communication and Computing Research Centre.

David informed me in May 2022 that he is now an emeritus professor.

David was brought up in the village of Fryston, Castleford. I was brought up, and live now, 6 minutes' walk from the first street in Fryston, South View. I first met David in 2011 when he videoed an interview with me for a DVD (based on a book, *Fryston – Its Life and Times*). He talked to many people who were associated with Fryston. With his advice and a grant from the National Lottery Heritage Fund and others, "Fryston Memories" began. This was a community website with photos, stories, etc.

David has published widely during his academic career. His latest book was published by Route Publishing in 2020: *Pit folks and Peers: The Remarkable History of the People of Fryston: Volume I – Echoes of Fryston Hall (1809-1908)* by David Waddington.

"In the first volume of a two-volume history of the pit village that raised him, David Waddington has dug deep to present with joy and relish the undiscovered history of Fryston Hall, which was, as he describes it, 'the most important hub of Victorian society outside of London, attracting the most eminent poets, writers, politicians, adventurers and other celebrities of the era.'

"Fryston-born David has written extensively on the sociology of mining communities, industrial relations in the British coal industry, the regeneration of former coal-mining areas, and the policing of political and industrial protest. One of his previous books, *Coal, Goals and Ashes: Fryston Colliery's Pursuit of the West Riding County FA Challenge Cup*, was published by Route in 2013."

http://www.route-online.com/authors/david-p-waddington.html accessed 23 12 21.

I am honoured that he has included me in some of his work in this area. We get on very well and he has been kind enough to quote me in the first volume of the book mentioned above. He is one of the two professors I know who have encouraged me with my new hobby of writing. He has made me realise how much history can be documented from remembering what people have said or communicating with them. I am amazed at the detailed social history David has written about the small part of the town of Castleford where I have lived for more than sixty years on and off.

David has asked me to write the foreword for the second volume, which will bring his historical record and analysis to a time when my parents and I lived and worked here. My father started work in Airedale in about 1922. When I was involved in training potential general practitioners there was a lot of emphasis on consultation and communication skills. I think most people who read this will agree that the body language David is displaying in the photograph shows he is a happy and friendly bloke.

If you read on, you will see that the professors I know well are all friendly with good senses of humour. Even though a professor may be eminent and world famous, he or she can be down-to-earth and not forget their roots.

Brian T. Colvin

Brian Colvin
Photo by Graham Hillman

Brian, his wife, Kathryn, and me at their Golden Wedding
Celebration, August 2021. Apothecaries Hall, London

It wasn't until I researched the internet for Brian that I discovered that he is the only friend of mine to have an entry in Debrett's. Below is a screenshot of the entry.

Birthdate 1946-01-17

Education Sevenoaks Sch, Clare Coll Cambridge (MA, MB BChir), London Hosp Med Coll

Publications N/A

Recreations foreign travel, opera, cricket

Clubs MCC

Style Prof Brian Colvin

Career conslt haematologist: St Peter's Hosp Gp and Inst of Urology 1977-86, Barts and the London NHS Tst 1977-2009, ret; dir of postgrad med and dental educn Royal Hosps Tst 1996-99, dean Queen Mary's Sch of Medicine and Dentistry 1998-2008, hon prof Queen Mary Univ of London, medical dir haemophilia Pfizer Europe 2008-; dir Clinical Pathology Accreditation Ltd 1998-2004; memb: Standing Ctee of Membs RCP 1973-77, Ctee Br Soc for Haematology 1983-86, Med Advsy Ctee Haemophilia Soc 1993-2007; chm: Haemostasis and Thrombosis Sub-Ctee BCSH 1991-94, Steering Ctee UK Nat External Quality Assurance Scheme (NEQAS) in Blood Coagulation 1992-96 and 2005-11, UK Haemophilia Centre Dirs Orgn 1993-96, Panel of Examiners in Haematology RCPath 1994-99, Nat Quality Assurance Advsy Panel in Haematology 1996-98, Ethics Ctee RCPath 2004-08; pres Cncl Pathology Section RSM 1996-98; pres Barts and The London Alumnus Assoc 2007-11; Queen Mary Univ of London Coll Medal 2012; Liveryman Worshipful Soc of Apothecaries; memb BMA; FRCPath 1988 (MRCPath 1976), FRCP 1990 (MRCP 1972), FRSM 1989-2008

Entry in Debrett's for Prof. Brian Colvin

We met as students at the London Hospital Medical College in 1966. We were to embark on our clinical studies, which involved being on the wards. Brian had spent three years undertaking preclinical studies in Cambridge. I had undertaken three years' preclinical studies at University College London. This included eighteen months studying anatomy for a BSc. Our clinical cohort at The London therefore included Oxbridge students, London BSc students and a group who had re-taken the second MB preclinical examinations because of failure of one or more elements. It was a fascinating group of people, some members of which became good friends of mine and we have kept in touch until the present day.

Brian and his wife, Kate, stayed with me for one night in June 2021. They live in London and were on their way to see friends who lived further north. It was a lovely stay, and I provided a simple evening meal. In one of the email exchanges which we made to arrange the visit, I posed a quiz question. "When was the last time I cooked a meal for you both?" They could not remember. It was when Felicity and I were married and lived in a flat on the Finchley Road, North London. I had roasted a duck. When I was carving at the table,

I unexpectedly came across a polythene bag full of stuff. I had no idea that when one buys such birds from the butcher, the giblets are put inside the fowl in a polythene bag. This was one of the many faux pas I have made in my lifetime. (The plural of faux pas is the same as the singular but is pronounced differently. The singular is pronounced "fou pa" and the plural, "fou paz".)

Brian and I were two of the few people from our year to continue working at the London Hospital Medical College after we qualified and undertook our house jobs. I became a lecturer in physiology, which was a teaching and research post. I left that post after three years to become a general practitioner in Cheltenham. Brian progressed in haematology and has had a stunning career as you can see from the CV above. He remained at the Royal London Hospital until he retired. Incidentally, his brother, Peter, was a consultant anaesthetist at The London until his retirement. Brian's wife, Kate, had an equally stunning career. She joined the Foreign Office in 1968 and was ambassador to the Holy See from 2002 to 2005.

"From 1999 to 2001 she was Her Majesty's Vice Marshal of the Diplomatic Corps, a senior member of the Royal Household and the Queen's link with the diplomatic community in London. The role involved arranging the annual Diplomatic Corps Reception by the Sovereign, organising the regular presentation of credentials ceremonies for Ambassadors and High Commissioners, and supervising attendance of diplomats at state events." Wikipedia accessed 15 5 22.

She still works, meeting and greeting heads of state and others visiting the UK. Brian and Kate are a thoughtful and kind couple, and I am sure this was reflected in their work. They have always been thoughtful and kind towards me and I greatly appreciate that.

In 2017 I wanted to invite relations of mine to come with me to the Royal Opera House, Covent Garden as a treat. Claire is a goddaughter of my late wife, Kath. Since her death in 2015 I have adopted Claire as my goddaughter. Claire's then sister-in-law, Obose, is Nigerian and at that time had never been to an opera. I decided on the light Donizetti opera, *L'elisir d'amore*. However, I was unable to get decent tickets on the internet. I remembered one of Brian's serious interests was opera and that he was a friend of Covent Garden and had priority when it comes to buying tickets. I cheekily asked if he could get me three good tickets for a concert in June and he did so. When I was in London it was decided that Kate would give me the tickets and I invited her to do that over a meal at Searcys St. Pancras Brasserie Restaurant. Brian was to be at an important committee meeting. After Kate and I had been chatting for a while, we were surprised to see Brian arriving at the restaurant. He told us that he had resigned from the committee that morning because he could not miss meeting me! What a charmer!

A group of us have been having a reunion associated with being at the London Hospital as students. The reunion has been taking place annually for decades, since before 1973. Two of these reunions took place in Rome and we stayed in the ambassador's residence. This was a magnificent facility. Kath and I could only make one and it was a fantastic experience. We had previously popped in and had a cuppa on the terrace with Brian and Kate on our way back from a holiday in Southern Italy.

Kath, Brian and Kate on the terrace, the residence of the ambassador to the Holy See

Herman Waldmann

Like Brian Colvin, Herman undertook his preclinical studies at Cambridge University. He was a fellow clinical student at the London Hospital Medical College. He is now the emeritus professor of pathology at the University of Oxford. He has had a stunning career.

"Waldmann was elected a Fellow of the <u>Royal Society</u> in 1990. He delivered the 1992 <u>Bradshaw Lecture</u> at the Royal College of Physicians. In 1998, he was a founding fellow of the <u>Academy of Medical Sciences</u>. In 2008, he was awarded an honorary doctorate ScD (Hon) by the University of Cambridge. In 2010 he became a Fellow of the Royal College of Physicians (FRCP). In 2005 he received the Jose Carreras award from the European Hematology Association and, the Excellence in Clinical Research Award from the Juvenile Diabetes Research Foundation. In 2007 he was awarded Thomas E Starzl Prize in Surgery and Immunology, and also, the Scrip Lifetime Achievement award from the pharmaceutical industry. He is an honorary fellow of Queen Mary Westfield College, and of both King's College and Sidney Sussex College, Cambridge. He is an honorary member of the <u>British Society for Immunology</u>." Wikipedia. Accessed 30th December 2021.

Being elected as a Fellow of the Royal Society is one of the very highest honours that can be bestowed on a scientist. He or she will have made a very substantial contribution to human knowledge. You will see what I mean when I tell you that past fellows of the

Royal Society include Isaac Newton, Charles Darwin, and Albert Einstein. In 2018 there were sixty fellows of the Royal Society who were also Nobel laureates.

Over the years, I have heard about Herman from mutual friends Graham Hillman and Steve Shalet. I meet them regularly and they have kept in touch with Herman. In September 2016 I went to the golden wedding celebration of Graham and Francine Hillman in Cambridge. I was at the same table as Herman and his wife. He was very kind to me about one of the books I had written which included quite a lot about when we were all students together. Two or three years ago we became Facebook friends. I don't know why, but I was rather surprised he used Facebook. He obviously has some high-powered scientific Facebook friends and there have been communications between them about Covid that are beyond me. However, like a lot of Facebook users, Herman publishes some daft things on the site.

Herman Waldmann

Facebook 31 12 21

Even the most eminent and famous professors have great senses of humour!

Stephen Shalet

Steve started as a preclinical medical student at the London Hospital Medical College in 1963, the same year as I started at UCL. We both did the extended course to obtain a BSc, Steve in physiology and I in anatomy. We met when I joined students at the London Hospital to undertake our clinical training as I mentioned above.

Steve knew his first wife, Carol, since they were 16 years old. My earliest memory of them is playing monopoly in Robin and Christine Harrod's flat (two other student friends). I was invited to their wedding, which took place in a synagogue. It was the first synagogue I had ever been in. We were issued with paper skullcaps and mine blew off at the start of the service. I think the draft of air was created by the incessant talking!

Meet Stephen Shalet the Society's
2021 Jubilee Medal Lecturer

"The Jubilee Medal is an occasional award made by gift of Council to a British endocrinologist to recognise outstanding contribution to endocrinology and to the Society*. The Medal was instituted to mark the 50th year of publication of the Journal of Endocrinology.

*Society of Endocrinology

"I completed a BSc in Physiology at London University and qualified in medicine at the Royal London Hospital. My medical training posts in London and Bristol were followed by an appointment as Research Fellow in Endocrinology at the Christie Hospital, Manchester. I formally retired in 2005 but carried on seeing patients until around 2010. Now all I really do is I teach, I like the subject, so it's not really work, it's enjoyable. Occasionally, I referee a paper and participate in data safety monitoring boards. I still do a moderate amount of that work, which keeps me in the loop in terms of what's going on in the field."

Lyndsey Forsyth. Interview. The Endocrine Post. Published 26/10/21. Accessed 2 1 22.

I could write a lot about Steve, but I will concentrate on our friendship, particularly our recent friendship. I cannot resist describing an encounter with Steve when we were both medical students. I had my twenty-first birthday party in my parents' GP surgery, which was semi-detached from the private house. My parents had a small gathering in the sitting room. Steve arrived a little late and accidentally went into the sitting room and asked, "Is there any of the hard stuff?" I think there was only cider and soft drinks available at the party.

His first wife, Carol, tragically died not many years ago. I really regret not to have been able to attend her funeral. When Steve retired and became an emeritus professor, he moved from Manchester to Edale in Derbyshire. He lived in a beautiful large apartment which was part of Edale Mill. This had been converted to many such units. He lived there with Barbara, his second wife. That marriage did not work out. Kath and I visited as it was not too far away.

After Kath died and Barbara had left, both Steve and I were living alone. He kindly invited me for a night to stay with him so we could have a good chat, which we did after he showed me round the beautiful area where the house was situated. The next morning, as I was leaving, Steve produced a framed photograph he had hidden in a cupboard near the entrance to the apartment. It was a photograph of him and the new love of his life, Diana. He had hidden it so that I wouldn't start asking who on earth she was. I was delighted. Steve and Diana are very happily married and have moved to a house in Sheffield which can accommodate their respective children and guests.

I really appreciate the close friendship that has developed between the three of us. We have stayed at one another's homes and on one occasion they invited me to join them for a couple of nights in a self-catering rented holiday flat near Ambleside. I stayed with them over Christmas in 2022. Steve's son, Daniel, was there over that Christmas and I was delighted to spend time with him. We got on well. He had inherited motor neuron disease. He inherited this from his mother, Carol, who was adopted. He had significant mobility and speech problems. Steve had looked after him like gold, as did Diana. He died after a very short illness in October 2023. I had the honour of being asked to read the poem I sent to Yvonne Crewe, which is in full in Chapter 1. I include a photo of him and me so that he will be remembered in a published book.

Daniel Shalet and me, 2022

Steve describes himself as a secular Jew. He was brought up in the East End of London, where his father was a general practitioner. My mother was Jewish and therefore so am I. However, neither my mother or I had any relationship with the Jewish religion, and I still do not know much about it. However, I do feel an empathy and connection with people and friends who have a Jewish heritage and I sense that the feeling is mutual. Steve has a fantastic sense of humour. A friend once asked me "What is a Jewish sense of humour?" and I could not answer immediately. Steve pointed out but that Jewish humour was significantly self-deprecating. It was obvious when I thought of Joan Rivers and Jackie Mason. I think I have a good sense of humour and I'm quite happy telling stories which are self-deprecating.

Diana also has a great sense of humour, and it is always fun when we three meet. We also have some fascinating discussions. Steve has encouraged me in my new hobby of writing and both he and Diana are motivating people.

Since I found out I was a distant relation (ninth cousin, twice removed) of Fred Astaire, Steve often calls me "twinkle toes". We had a lovely meeting for lunch at the Yorkshire Sculpture Park and when we were leaving and at the car park, Steve started dancing and singing "putting on your top hat". There were people about! They probably thought it was time for him to return to the ward at Fieldhead Hospital, Wakefield, part of the mental health trust of South West Yorkshire.

Another time, I told them about when Harry Corbett came to my sixth birthday party and performed magic with the original Sooty. (I don't think Sweep was around in those days!) I even have a photograph from that day. It was taken in the waiting room of the surgery.

Sooty and Harry Corbett at my birthday party
Photo – Photographer, Jack Hulme

I invited Steve and Diana out on one occasion to the Wentbridge House brasserie. I think it might have been to celebrate my birthday in 2000. Suddenly, two puppets were revealed, and I think 'Happy Birthday' was sung.

Sweep, Steve, Sooty and Diana
To quote a friend of mine, Gill: "Barking!"

Diana Greenfield

Steve and Diana married in 2019. Fancy knowing a married couple of profs!!

Diana Greenfield

"I am currently Consultant Nurse and Multidisciplinary Team Lead in Late Effects (of cancer treatment) in Specialised Cancer Services at Sheffield Teaching Hospital NHS Foundation Trust and Honorary Professor in Cancer Survivorship in the Department of Oncology and Metabolism. For over a decade, I have led a multi-disciplinary team for survivors of cancer, a relatively new clinical field. Striving to keeping research close to the patient, I am committed to the cycle of practice-generating research questions and research to inform practice. In the last three years I have an accrued grant income of over £3 million as lead and co-applicant, and with over 70 publications in peer-reviewed journals and book chapters.

"At the heart of my clinical practice is the commitment to delivering compassionate, evidence-based, person-centred holistic care. I strongly believe that empowering clinical academics in clinical leadership positions will seek dividends in terms of excellence in patient care and improved clinical outcomes. I believe my service is testament to that. My clinical team have been recognised nationally in the prestigious Health Service Journal/Nursing Times Awards as Cancer Care Team of the year (2014). I was further awarded "Inspirational Leader" of the year by the Yorkshire and Humber NHS Leadership Academy and was a finalist in the national NHS Leadership Academy. I was also commended for a Macmillan Excellence Award in Innovation in 2016. These awards are in recognition of excellence in service innovation and delivery of care."

University of Sheffield Website. Accessed 4 1 22.

Towards the end of May 2022, the following was announced on Facebook:

> "A consultant nurse has become an honorary professor at both of the city's universities in recognition of her clinical and academic contribution to nursing. Professor Diana Greenfield, who works at Sheffield Teaching Hospitals NHS Foundation Trust and leads the cancer late effects multi-disciplinary team, has added an honorary professorship at Sheffield Hallam University (SHU) to the one she already held at the University of Sheffield."

What an amazing achievement.

Diana's father was a distinguished business statistician and visiting professor to the University of Newcastle-upon-Tyne. Her mother, Sheila, was the founding principle of Legan College, Castlereagh, Northern Ireland. It was the first formally integrated school, and she received an MBE for her work. I hope to meet her over Christmas 2023.

Diana takes after her father in that she is a left-wing radical. She is a humanist and is quite polite about my Catholicism. It is good that she is a Facebook friend of mine. Her Facebook entries demonstrate to me what a good mother she is. Facebook also illustrates what great sense of humour she has. She and her mother are also Facebook friends with one another.

John Lord

John Lord

From 1997 to 2006 John was a Yorkshire GP tutor and this is how I met him. I was a GP tutor from 1992 and then an associate director of postgraduate education at the Yorkshire Deanery to 2004. We regularly met at residential development seminars based mainly at the York and St. John Teacher Training College in Ripon. It was a wonderful experience and our leader, Dr. Jamie Bahrami, the Director of Postgraduate General Practice Education, was one of my heroes. GP tutors each looked after the postgraduate education and development of general practitioners in the area where they worked. I was the GP tutor for the Pontefract district and John for Huddersfield.

In 1999 he became Honorary Professor of Primary Medical Care at Huddersfield University. He developed an MSc course for prospective nurse practitioners. For two years I was the supervisor of Jackie Spencer, our district nurse, who undertook the course.

Primary care education was John's speciality. Below is a quote of the recommendations from a salient paper he wrote.

"Key Recommendations

1. More clinical work and more education could and should occur in primary care, but resources must genuinely follow diverted activity.
2. The HR crisis in primary care needs addressing now, partly by training NPs [nurse practitioners] and PAs [physician assistants], and partly by centralisation of services.
3. Systems thinking can promote a culture of trust and honesty, both with patients and with colleagues.
4. Patients, not managers, should set the quality agenda. To achieve this patients need the opportunity to be involved.
5. As an absolute minimum, 10% (a tithe) of professional time should be in self/team development.
6. Simple evidence-based adjustment to educational techniques could easily be adopted in primary care."

From – Lord, John R (2003) The Future of Primary Healthcare Education. *Postgraduate Medical Journal* (79). pp. 553-560.

The most important recommendation as far as I am concerned is number 5. Having time to reflect on one's work has largely disappeared and is, in my opinion, responsible for a major recruitment problem made worse by the Covid pandemic.

John has a fantastic sense of humour. Round about Christmas time, there was an annual meeting for course organisers and GP tutors at the end of a development seminar in Ripon. The seminar ended on their last evening with a Christmas dinner with quite a lot of alcohol. On one occasion, John set up an elaborate task for us. We were each supplied with a small glass – a shot glass. There must have been thirty of us.

Each of us in turn had to pour some water into our shot glass and then add it to a tower created by these glasses. The tower was positioned on the table right in front of where the director, Jamie Bahrami, was seated. it was a delicate exercise, and one false move could bring all the glasses of water down to spill on the boss's nether regions. We liked the boss so much that we did not fail to build a stable structure!

I attended his inaugural lecture after John had been appointed a professor at Huddersfield University. He is a fantastic speaker, and this lecture was peppered with most amusing anecdotes and slides.

Another tradition was that when a long-standing educationalist retired from his or her post a posh dinner was put on with postprandial speeches. I was honoured to have one such dinner for me when I retired as an associate director of postgraduate general practise education, Yorkshire. It took place in Weetwood Hall on the outskirts of Leeds. I made a speech as did the director, George Taylor. However, the highlight speech was John Lord's, which brought the house down. At the end of it he presented me with a DVD of all the amusing cartoons he had collected over the years. To this day he sends out amusing cartoons and videos regularly and below this is one he sent towards the end of 2021.

fwd. To whoever it was who told me to leave my car at the pub and take the bus.....

. . . turns out I was in no fit state to drive that either.

Sir Norman Williams

"**Professor Sir Norman Stanley Williams** <u>FRCS FRCP FRCPE</u> <u>FMedSci FRCA</u> (born 15 March 1947) is a British surgeon and former President of the <u>Royal College of Surgeons of England</u> (2011–14).[1] He was <u>knighted</u> in the <u>2015 New Year Honours</u>.[2]

"He was educated at <u>Roundhay School, Leeds</u> and the London Hospital Medical College. His surgical training was in London, Bristol, Leeds and UCLA, Los Angeles, USA where he went as a Fulbright scholar in 1980. In 1982 he was appointed Senior Lecturer/Honorary Consultant Surgeon at the University of Leeds and the Leeds General Infirmary. He subsequently was appointed to the Chair of Surgery at his alma mater in 1986 and in 1995 became the Head of the merged Academic Department of Surgery of Barts and The London School of Medicine and Dentistry, Queen Mary, University of London, and Honorary Consultant Colorectal Surgeon at The Royal London Hospital. His main clinical interests have revolved around sphincter saving procedures and his scientific endeavours have concentrated on gastrointestinal pathophysiology." Wikipedia. Accessed 7 1 22

Norman Williams

I know Norman very much less well than the others. Norman is slightly younger than I and was at the London Hospital at the same time. My friends in Cheltenham, Bill and Anna Bullingham, invited Kath and me for a weekend. Bill was very much involved with the National Centre for Bowel Research based at the London Hospital. Norman became its director. Bill raised a lot of charity money for that unit where he met Norman. Norman and his wife, Linda, were also invited for that weekend. That is the only significant social contact I have made with Norman. However, he is a very kind man. He took the trouble to write me a nice letter after Kath died.

Last year one of my friends, Mike Dawson, who was an orthopaedic surgeon in the USA and who was in the same year as me at the London Hospital, died. I was asked to say something at a memorial event held in the library of the Royal College of Surgeons on 31 October 2021. I asked Norman if he would kindly write a paragraph for me to read out at the end of my bit. What he wrote created a very poignant moment at that event.

Eric Teasdale

Professor Eric L. Teasdale

Eric became a doctor and pursued a career in occupational medicines, becoming a consultant occupational physician. He had a very successful career, and the pinnacle was his appointment as Chief Medical Officer (global health and well-being) of the pharmaceutical company AstraZeneca UK. I think we all may well have heard of that company!

Eric is younger than me and attended the same school as me and his brother, Colin. Colin and I were in the sixth form together, started at London University in digs together, shared a flat together and have remained good friends all the years since. I never really knew Eric very well but must have met him many times when I visited his parents' house in Wakefield to see Colin.

In 2021 and 2022 I was more in touch with Eric than ever. Colin developed multiple sclerosis many years previously and this progressed very slowly. In the years just mentioned, he has had four hospital admissions with aspiration pneumonia. Each time he was very seriously ill. Eric contacted me after he had visited his brother on the second occasion to tell me how very ill he was. Colin has always been strong-willed and stubborn. He fought his way back from each of these admissions to return home to be looked after by Anne, his wife.

The other time Eric contacted me was when he discovered that our biology master (or was he our zoology master?), Brian Fletcher, had died. Dr. Fletcher was an amazing teacher at QEGS. He was our mentor when we were sixth-formers and after. Both Eric and I went to see Dr. Fletcher for advice about our university careers and in both our cases his advice was life changing. Eric wrote a very good article in the school magazine about Dr. Fletcher.

One thing amuses me now about Eric. He mentioned that he was a volunteer giving Covid vaccinations. I wonder how he feels putting Pfizer vaccinations into people's arms! I'm glad we have got one another's email addresses.

Martin Smith

Martin Smith

Martin is slightly younger than I am. He is the half-nephew of my late wife Kath. She and Martin had known one another since they were kids. Martin, and his family, have been close friends of ours for many decades and remain dear friends of mine now. He and his wife, Jennifer, live not so many miles away in Leeds. Their daughter, Claire, was Kath's goddaughter, and I have adopted Claire as my goddaughter since Kath died in 2015. I asked Martin if he would write something for me about how he became a professor, and this follows.

"My Romanian adventure began in 1997 when Julian Rusu sought to further his studies for his PhD while instigating an EU Tempus grant, the aims of which were: 'to facilitate the restructuring of the higher education sector in central and eastern European countries through inter-university cooperation'.

"Manfred Bochman my head of department in the Inorganic section of the School of Chemistry at the University of Leeds, invited Julian to share my office. I paid a reciprocal visit to Julian's university in May/June of that year and presented two seminars describing respectively, the structure of chemistry courses at Leeds and the use of videos in chemistry teaching.

"In April/May of 1998 I was invited by Julian's department, (Inorganic Chemistry, Faculty of Industrial Chemistry, Gheorghe Asachi Technical University of Iasi), as an official referee for the examination of Julian's PhD thesis: 'Oxide Type Compounds with Special Properties'. Towards the end of March 1999, I was invited to Iasi to contribute to the workshop: 'Modularisation and the European Credit Transfer System', again with the support of a Tempus grant.

"In 2001 I was invited to Iasi to receive an Honorary Professorship from the Faculty of Industrial Chemistry for 'Special Merit in the Field of Collaboration'. On that occasion I gave a lecture entitled: 'Practical Classes for the Delivery of Value and Values in Chemical Higher Education'."

M. J. Smith
BSc Hons Sheffield, 1967
D Phil Oxon, 1971
Thesis title: 'The Role of Transition Metals in the Reactions of Co-ordinated Ligands.'

Martin is one of the most modest people I have ever come across. I think he only mentions this professorship within the family.

Peter Garlick

Peter and I went to school together in Wakefield, and we were close friends then. I kept in touch with him when he was at Cambridge and when he worked for a while at St. Mary's Hospital London. We completely lost touch after that. Another school friend, David Holmes, told me about Peter occasionally and informed me of Peter's untimely death in 2018. Peter is the second professor mentioned in this chapter who went to the same school as I. It would interest me to know how many professors there were who were in the same sixth form science year at the school as me.

Peter Garlick

"Peter had a brilliant scientific mind, which was evident throughout his career in protein metabolism research. Among countless academic achievements was his contribution to the field of human nutritional protein requirements as the chair of the Protein Subgroup for the U.S. National Academy of Sciences and serving as an expert consultant for the World Health Organization, for which he was very proud.

"He saw the world around him through the eyes of a scientist. He was a true scholar, always learning, discovering and figuring out how things worked. As a researcher, truths had to be proven through careful examination of evidence.

"He loved the natural world, particularly the weather, trees, and birds. He loved collecting and analyzing meteorological data. He also collected seeds and saplings of trees (somewhat covertly) from all over the world to plant in his gardens."

News-Gazette.com. Accessed 26 1 22

The last sentence in the above obituary brought back a memory of Peter. When we were in our mid-teens, he was interested in identifying trees from the leaves. I also got interested in that with him but never took it forward. Peter lived in Queens Drive, Ossett, Wakefield. His father was the borough water engineer and used the method of water divining to find the pipes, etc. Of course, Peter and I had to have a go at this. I don't think we were very successful.

I developed a hobby of two-way radio transmission. Once a week, I stayed the night with my Uncle Sam and Auntie Agnes in Wakefield. That was when I had to attend scouts at our school. Peter's House was about 1.5 miles from my uncle's. I took my walkie-talkie equipment and lent Peter a receiver/transmitter. It was very difficult to connect at that distance and I am sure the crackly sounds drove our relations mad.

Earlier in Peter's career, when we were both in London, he was doing some experiments on rats at St Mary's Hospital, London. I was a clinical medical student at the time and somehow had got interested in kidney surgery from a theoretical point of view. Professor Blandy (see below) encouraged me in this interest. Peter supervised me removing one kidney in an anaesthetised rat to see later what happened to the other kidney.

When we were students, Peter, I, and others met up either in London or Cambridge. On one occasion Peter invited me to a dinner at

St John's College, Cambridge. The College has a license from the Queen which allows cooked swan to be eaten. Swan was on the menu. It was a grand occasion. Whenever I visited Cambridge a small wave of envy came over me as it had such a superb learning environment.

2. Professors with whom I have worked

I worked closely with two professors when I was in London. The first was J. Z. Young, with whom I worked as an undergraduate in the department of anatomy, University College London. The second was W. R. Keatinge who was my PhD supervisor when I was a lecturer in physiology at the London Hospital Medical College. Both of those men became heroes of mine and remain so now. I wrote about them in my book published in 2012, *The English Doctor*. Here, I will write about them here from a different perspective.

"JZ" Young

J. Z. Young

Usually referred to as "JZ", John Zachary Young was the professor of anatomy at University College London, where I started as a medical student in 1963. He was appointed professor in 1945. He was a zoologist and the first non-medical person to take up that post. Indeed, I did not realise he was not a doctor for a good couple of weeks after I started! After eighteen months, twelve of us took time out from medical training, to study a BSc in Anatomy with him and I got to know him well. He is one of the heroes who influenced my life, and it was a great honour to be studying and working closely with such an eminent scientist.

The heading of his obituary in *The Guardian* on Monday 14 July 1997 was "Broad grasp of the brain". I keep the obituary cutting prominently in my study. Here is a quote:

> "His Gifford lectures embrace physiology, coding and communication, revolution and was at that time, at the cutting edge of molecular genetics ... This is science in the grand manner, and like that of the great Victorians, built on revolutionary perceptions, a huge grasp and great courage ... he became the 1928–29 Oxford scholar at the Naples zoological station ... It was there, studying the autonomous nervous system of fish, Young investigated the tube like structures which serve the muscles driving the squids' jet propulsion system ... Young showed that they are giant nerve fibres. .... at the time of his death, he was working with Marion Nixon on an entirely new book on the cephalopods."

He was the third BBC Reith lecturer in 1950. His lecture was entitled "Doubt and certainty in science". It seems to be one of the very few Reith lectures which is not available as a BBC podcast. However, there is a transcript available at https://www.bbc.co.uk/radio4/features/the-reith-lectures/transcripts/1948/ (accessed 25 10 23). I possess the book he authored based on the lectures. I don't know where he found the time, but he also wrote textbooks for schools. I possess two of these: *The Life of Vertebrates and The Life of Mammals*. I came across them in second-hand bookshops over the years.

One could guess from what I have written about him above, that JZ's influence on the London University curriculum for the BSc in Anatomy would result in us being taught in a non-paternalistic fashion how to think about science. The curriculum was divided into several areas including comparative embryology, anthropology, and histology. There were about twenty others in the University of London studying for this degree and sometimes we were taught together. My friend from school, Colin Teasdale, undertook his BSc in Anatomy at the London Hospital Medical College. I made friends with two of his fellow students, Robin Harrod and Adrian Bomford. Robin was the best man at my first wedding. Their professor of anatomy was called Harrison and at one point he dissected a whale on the roof of the medical school.

JZ adopted the Oxford tutorial system. This was a one-to-one teaching method. This involved his setting an essay to be written. On completion, it was handed in to him to read and comment on. One was then faced with a meeting with him in his study to discuss the work. The first time, I was frightened to death but as time went on, I realised that was a ridiculous feeling. He was a kind man and one of the big things I learned from him was not to talk down to people. There was a mutual respect despite his eminence. In the years I worked as a scientist I noticed that this was a trait in most eminent scientists I came across.

During the summer holiday our group was split into two groups of six. Each group worked with JZ in the Naples zoological station for six weeks. We worked in the laboratory with JZ and other scientists he had invited. For some reason unknown to me, the research was funded by the United States Air Force. This is not the place for me to describe the research with which I was involved there. I want to stick to describing the man and my relationship with him.

He made sure we experienced Naples and its environs. We worked from 8 a.m. to 12 noon and then 4 p.m. to 8 p.m. Often in the afternoons he drove us to somewhere of interest such as Herculaneum. He had his own large estate car which he drove from the UK. That seated six. Sometimes we were taken somewhere to swim. In the evenings we ate out, mostly sitting outside. The food was great, and we had plenty of wine. Sometimes JZ would take us out for a meal and would pay for us all. On one occasion (I think it was towards the end of our six weeks) he took us to his favourite restaurant. There was a small orchestra and when the musicians saw JZ entering, they struck up his favourite tune – "Come back to Sorrento". We sometimes swam in the evening when it was dark. He often lent us his car. No one seemed to bother about speed limits or restricting alcohol intake when driving in Naples. One evening, when JZ was driving us somewhere to eat, a policeman stopped him for some reason. JZ wound the car window down and told the policeman to "F... off" and then drove off at speed.

Our expenses were paid and three of us lived in a small, rented flat. For breakfast we had a croissant and coffee at a bar on the way to work. Lots of working people breakfasted like this in Italy. We were allowed to have a two-day break and do anything we fancied. We were split up into pairs for this. JZ gave us a handful of cash to spend. I went with Dave Bromham by train and boat to Sicily. To save a bit of money we stayed the night on a bench in Palermo railway station. We were glad to get back to Naples.

I drove JZ's car back to the UK from Naples. I think there were three or four of us in the car with our luggage and scientific instruments in the back. One piece of equipment was an automatic octopus feeding device. When the UK customs asked (at 2 a.m.) whether we had anything to declare, I mentioned the feeding device as a bit of a joke. The customs officer did not smile and asked us to take it out for him to have a look. I was not popular with my friends for delaying a rather tiring journey.

Our final BSc examination results were given to us by JZ in the Marlborough, Arms which is just off Gower Street. I obtained the lower second-class degree. JZ apologised to me and told me he had fought for an upper second for me at the examination meeting. I have never worried about getting a lower second. Robin Harrod and Colin Teasdale (friends mentioned above) received first-class degrees. Adrian Bomford also obtained a lower second. It is interesting that he and I ended up doing research and the other two, clinical jobs.

Studying with JZ was a profound experience for me. Amongst other things, he taught me to question without being cynical. JZ is one of the reasons why I was regarded by some ex-colleagues as a polymath and with a Socratic teaching style. Was he my friend? No. However, his guidance, supervision and socialising were very friendly experiences. It was his close working and teaching relationship with me that was life changing. He was a gentle giant.

JZ was 90 years old when he died. I hope that when I am 90, I will still be doing some unpaid voluntary work of interest as well as some writing.

William R. Keatinge

Bill Keatinge

I was in bed for the job interview with Bill Keatinge. It was a hospital bed in the private wing of the London Hospital. I was recovering from an operation for a pilonidal sinus undertaken by Mr. Alan Parks. (He was a colorectal surgeon who later in his stunning career became president of the Royal College of Surgeons and a knight.)

One of the questions Bill asked me was whether I was proposing to be a perpetual student. I knew what he meant. He meant whether I was prepared to undertake a job of work but at the same time continue to learn. The job was a lecturer in physiology. It was a teaching and research job. At that time, Bill was the reader in physiology at the London Hospital Medical College. I was pleased to be offered the job, which I accepted. It was a drop in salary from that of a house officer. I write more about the science I undertook with him in Chapter 5. I want to write about Bill the person with whom I worked for three years. He was an expert on aspects of hypothermia.

He died in April 2008. The following are quotes from *The Times* obituary on 8 May of that year.

"Professor W.R. (Bill) Keatinge

Scientist who showed that denizens of temperate climes are more likely to die of heat or cold than those in torrid or icy zones.

"In the early 1980s, the media shocked society reporting that in Britain, 100,000 elderly people chill to death in their homes every winter. The conventional wisdom was that that they died of hypothermia ... But these deaths were not due to hypothermia. Heart attacks and strokes were the cause of most of these deaths, with respiratory illnesses being responsible for most of the rest ... Keatinge's research involving experiments on volunteers showed normal adjustment by the body and mild cold was to blame.

"He retired in 1995 and was made an emeritus professor. But he continued his active career until a few weeks before his death.

"Keatinge collaborated with many scientists from several countries, and he developed particularly close links with Russia. He was fascinated with the Russian language and learned to speak it well enough to be understood on his visit to the country."

When I started work in the physiology department towards the end of 1970, I was immediately befriended by Jeffrey Graham, who was working on his PhD with Bill. They were working on the neural system of pigs' arteries. I have kept in touch with Jeff over the years but, more recently, he gave me a very precious book. It is a privately published book written by Bill and titled *College in the East End*. The book describes in detail his visits to undertake research in

Russia. Also described in detail is his involvement in the merger of The London, Barts and Queen Mary in the University of London. It is a rare and precious possession of mine. Jeff enclosed a letter asking me to leave this book in my will to the Royal Society of Medicine Library. I have informed my executors and beneficiaries where the book is kept.

Bill was one of the kindest, friendliest and most polite persons I have ever come across. I was allowed to spend two or three months seeing what research was going on in the physiology department and could choose with whom I would like to work. What an amazing luxury! I was warned that Bill could be difficult. Looking back on that comment, I think it was office gossip and I never personally experienced his being difficult. I chose to work with Bill because I got interested in human physiology and his work on hypothermia and survival in cold water. He always let me explore my own ideas.

We had a significant meeting together about every two weeks, but I could always pop in and have a chat and ask a question. We could also chat during the morning coffee break.

He was another scientist who never spoke down to me. "Behaviour breeds behaviour." He and J. Z. Young taught me a lot of how to communicate with others.

Once a year he held a party at his rather smart house in Roehampton. There was a trampoline in the garden which was very popular. He invited technicians, PhD students and members of academic staff. It was tradition to serve a curry at that event.

I once stayed at his house on the night before we were to drive to Oxford from me to present our work to the Physiological Society. I was a heavy smoker at that time and was dreading the night at Bill's because I would not be able to smoke. What I did not know what is that his wife, Annette, was also a heavy smoker. I was pleased that when I was shown by her to my bedroom, she had put an ashtray out for me next to the bed.

After my first marriage broke down, I resigned my general practice job in Cheltenham and Bill went to a lot of trouble to get me my job back as a lecturer in physiology at the London Hospital Medical College. The job started shortly after Kath and I married. I worked there for about three weeks and decided I did not like it at all. I didn't have the guts to tell Bill to his face and phoned him up. I really had let him down. I continued to meet Bill in London after I settled with Kath in Yorkshire. He remained a friend of mine until the day he died. If I wanted to ask anything about clinical thermometers, I would email him. When forehead strips were first manufactured to be used in diagnosing fever by a change in colour related increasing forehead skin temperature, I emailed him for his opinion. Personally, I thought these were rubbish. He sent me a simple reply: "pretty colours!!" I wonder what he would've thought of forehead temperature measurement as an indicator of Covid infection in the early days of the pandemic! I never heard him swear, but he might have done about that.

Jeffrey Graham and I put on a dinner for him at the Royal Society of Medicine in London. We invited as many people who had undertaken PhDs with Bill as supervisor as we could find. He was absolutely thrilled. My wife, Kath, came. She was bored out of her brains especially when a photograph was passed round the dinner table. It was of a fat Russian man who had survived in cold water for a very long time. Theoretically, he should have died. Bill was so pleased with that dinner that he invited us all back a couple of years later and paid for the lot of us. Kath stayed at home!

Bill is one of my lifetime heroes. His son is called Richard and is a general practitioner in Holyhead. Bill and I had a relationship of mutual respect and that his son was a GP was a factor in Bill's understanding me, I am sure.

I have a Google blog and write under the pseudonym of Professor Pavlov. (profpavlov.blogspot.com). There is a long piece I wrote about Bill on one of the three blogs I manage. Below is it a comment I had from his son.

Richard Keatinge said…

Googling my father's name, I found your page and read it with great pleasure. I might have met you briefly, but I guess you may want to know that Bill K is in his last few days or hours of life. Please contact me (dr.richard@Billslastname.net) if I can tell you any more.

Bill died in 2008. I miss him. I am sure it will be comfortably warm for him in heaven rather than unbearably red hot in the other place. I am sure that Jeff, like me, regards Bill as a friend. It was the close collaboration in research that is the catalyst for a good friendship.

Richard Baker

Richard Baker

Professor Richard Baker OBE MD FRCGP, FRCP

"I am a GP researcher, having been a general practitioner first in Cheltenham followed by Leicester City, and an academic at Bristol and then Leicester Universities. Head of Department at Leicester, 2003-2010. Now retired, I continue to undertake some academic activities. I have conducted research into patient experience of general practice, interventions to improve the quality of care, development of guidelines (with NICE), continuity of care and the outcomes of primary health care. On occasions, I have undertaken investigations of patterns of mortality at the request of senior NHS staff. The effect of primary health care in influencing population mortality is often taken for granted but the importance of this effect and the mechanisms that explain it are not well understood. The evidence that follows is based on my particular interest in primary health care and mortality." (from Evidence submitted to the Health and Social Care Select Committee, 2021).

My first GP job was in Cheltenham in the early 1970s. I was a partner in the Leckhampton Road practice. I worked there about four years. The first trainee was Richard Baker and his trainer in the practice was my friend, Robin Harrod. I left the practice after my divorce and I worked with Richard for a rather short time, just over six months. He took over my partnership. I undertook a research project there on febrile convulsions in children. The other piece of research I undertook was the construction of the Royal College of General Practitioners' age/sex register for the practice. With a research assistant, Dawn Adams, I published a paper of the cost and advantages of creating an age/sex register. Occasionally, over the years, I have contacted Richard and he has been kind enough to say that I had an influence on him regarding research. I think he was just being polite! He did some significant work for the college in developing a method of GPs being awarded the Fellowship the Royal College of General Practitioners by assessment. I met him once and confessed that I was ashamed that I had been awarded the fellowship by nomination! Richard has had a stunning career as an academic GP and continues to work as an emeritus professor at Leicester University.

3. Professors who taught me when I was a student

As medical students we were taught by many professors. I will mention just two from each of University College London, and the London Hospital Medical College. Each possessed quite different teaching styles but, nevertheless, I learned a lot from each one. I highly respected the ones I have chosen below.

Andrew Huxley

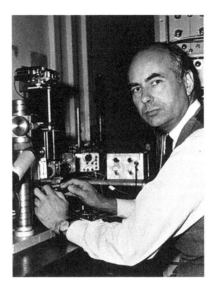

Extract from obituary in *The Guardian*, 2012:

"As a scientist, he possessed unusual breadth which, allied to practical gifts, enabled him to design and make essential and highly specialised experimental equipment. These skills underpinned his pioneering research into nerve function and muscle structure. Huxley was a collaborator and lifelong friend of Sir Alan Hodgkin, and succeeded him as master of Trinity in 1984. they shared the Nobel prize for physiology or medicine in 1963 for unravelling the biophysical mechanism of the nerve impulse."

Professor Huxley was the professor of physiology at University College London. He was a very boring lecturer. We counted how many times he said "erm" in a one-hour lecture. The details of how nerves worked was seriously complex for me and I'm not sure I have ever understood them. I remember him sticking an electrode into one of his forearm muscles during a lecture. The electrode was connected to an oscilloscope with a loudspeaker and somehow electrical impulses in the nerves could be heard and seen on the scope screen. Six of us had him as our tutor for one term. He marked our practical workbooks and then we discussed the experiments we did in the practical class. We met in his study. He knew the log tables by heart. He learned Russian in six weeks to prepare for a lecture tour there. I never heard him say anything amusing. We somewhat dreaded his boring lectures. That was before he won the Nobel Prize.

When the prize was announced he immediately became a hero. Loads of students stood outside his office window and shouted for him to appear, which he did to great vocal acclaim. From that time onwards he was a star. His lectures were packed and not just with medical students. We hung on to his every word. As I implied above, he talked with a rather monotonous voice. His words became exciting, and we shared in his experience of a major scientific discovery.

When I was working as a physiologist, I had to demonstrate one of my experiments at the Physiological Society. The equipment had to be transported to Oxford and set up. The experimental subject was Adrian Jacobs, one of the senior technicians. His legs were immersed in a tank full of coldish water and he exercised them by his feet working a pedal device inside the base of the tank. This pumped cooler blood to the rest of the body and lowered deep body temperature. Eminent scientists could wander round and ask questions of the demonstrators. I saw Andrew Huxley wandering into our room and I became seriously anxious that he would come and question me. He did ask a question and thank goodness it was not difficult to answer. Phew.

Bill Keatinge occasionally sent his draft scientific papers to Professor Huxley for comments.

S. Prakash Datta

Prof. P. Datta

"Prakash read first Chemistry at University College London (UCL) and then Medicine at University College Hospital Medical School in the early 1940s. Following this, he joined the academic staff of the Department of Biochemistry at UCL, becoming Professor of Medical Biochemistry in 1966 and acted as Head of the Biochemistry Department during 1969–1970. He subsequently had important roles in UCL as Dean of the Faculty of Medical Sciences (now Life Sciences) and as Vice-Provost between 1973 and 1978."

FEBS Federation of European Biochemical Societies. Online Letters 2010 https://febs.onlinelibrary.wiley.com/doi/full/10.1016/j.febslet.2010.07.051

Dr. Datta became a professor in my last year at University College London. I think one can tell from both the cartoon and a picture that he had a twinkling sense of humour and was a character.

There was a strong rumour that went round the medical students about Dr. Datta. He had designed an experiment which required a piece of equipment that included an element of rubber. Dr. Datta walked very slowly as though he was in a bit of a dream. A student saw him walking to a pharmacy in the Tottenham Court Road. There he bought 500 Durex condoms, took them back to the laboratory and cut the ends off for the experiment.

John Blandy

Professor Blandy was appointed a consultant surgeon at the London Hospital in 1964 and quickly specialised in urology. In 1969 he was appointed to the first departmental chair of urology in London.

"His output of research papers is legendary. He wrote in a style that encouraged readership and did many of the illustrations himself. His books were all medical best-sellers and strongly influenced his students and trainees. Most UK medical students learnt their urology from his Lecture notes in urology (Oxford, Blackwell Scientific). Many of today's consultants did their research in his department and owe their careers to his unstinting support.

"In the New Year honours of 1995, the Queen appointed him CBE for services to surgery. He was awarded the St Peter's medal of BAUS in 1982 and the Willy Grégoir medal of the Société Internationale d'Urologie in 2001.

"Both in working life and in retirement, he was a fine painter and sculptor. It was easy to know when a committee meeting had become too long as he would get out his pad and quietly sketch his fellow sufferers. At dinner in the RCS, he used to tour the portraits with other guests, give a learned critique of the artist and a life history of the subject. He died on 23 July 2011 from a sarcoma."

Royal College of Surgeons of England. Plarr's Lives of the Fellows. 2011

I mentioned in chapter 2, writing about Peter Garlick, that Prof. Blandy encouraged me to investigate a question I had asked him. Why does one kidney enlarge in size when the other one is removed? He arranged for the radiology department to get me X-rays from his operations before and after he had undertaken a removal of one kidney (a nephrectomy). He also showed me how to use a special instrument for measuring kidneys on X-rays. He arranged for me to use a small, quiet room after I had finished my day's work. I read up about the research and theories about this subject. I did not really get anywhere with an answer. On reflection I felt this was an amazing thing to do for a medical student. I have a research bug and, like J. Z. Young, he was a factor for my wanting to undertake some research after I had finished my house jobs.

Prof. Blandy was a talented artist. Writing about Bill Keatinge above, I mentioned the operation I had, conducted by Mr. Alan Parks. John Blandy painted him when he was President of the Royal College of Surgeons.

Painting of Mr. Alan Parks by John Blandy.
Displayed at The Hunterian Museum,
Royal College of Surgeons, England

Israel Doniach

Prof. Israel Doniach.
From St. Bartholomew's Hospital
Museum and Archive

Professor Doniach was one of many amazing teachers we had at the London Hospital Medical College. He was professor of morbid anatomy and head of the pathology department.

"The gentle kindly appearance of Professor Doniach, known as 'Sonny' to family and friends, and 'Do' to colleagues, was allied to a powerful scholarly intellect. He had a deceptively innocent but potentially devastating debating style involving the use of a simple question to drive a coach and horses through the adversarial argument. Conversation would nonetheless be punctuated by his keen sense of humour. Even shortly before his death, he responded to a joke with spontaneously hearty laughter. His compassion for others and his broad appreciation of scientific issues made him a much-revered teacher and university department head as scores of his pupils and colleagues would testify."

Royal College of Physicians, London. Inspiring Physicians.

History.rcplondon.ac.uk accessed 19 2 22.

There was a period when as clinical medical students we had to attend post-mortem teaching sessions. This was in the mid-1960s. These sessions took place in the middle of the day. Professor Doniach was in the background. The first one I attended was a patient who had died from carcinoma of the stomach. The house officer who looked after the patient on the wards presented the case in a formal way. The pathologist who had undertaken the post-mortem (autopsy) presented the findings. We were all struck by the number of findings at the post-mortem that were not discovered when the patient was alive. Professor Doniach asked the houseman one of his simple questions. The question was: "Tell me the dietary history of this patient. What did he have to eat?" Taking a dietary history was not part of the formal questioning. The junior doctor was silent. I have never forgotten that and tried to ask patients what they put into their stomachs when there was suspected gastric cancer. Professor Doniach visited patients on the wards who were in a terminal state. He did not tell them he was the pathologist, of course. He maintained it was useful to meet them before and after death.

Another post-mortem teaching session I remember vividly was that of a tramp from the streets of the East End of London. There were many tramps near the London Hospital when I was a student and one of their habits was drinking methylated spirits. This was a blue liquid that could easily be bought from various outlets. East End tramps thought that it was the blue chemical associated with the methylated spirit that was poisonous. One way of getting rid of the blue colour was by filtering the meths through a loaf of bread. The blue dye was harmless. This patient had been drinking meths, lit a cigarette, causing an explosion in the main bronchi (breathing tubes) of his lungs. This killed him. The pathologist who did the post-mortem held up the lungs to show the black charring of those tubes. I don't know whether this sort of teaching was common in other medical schools.

We were also taught what diseases looked like both with pathology specimens and examining histology tissues with a microscope. In my opinion this teaching brought us nearer to the subject, the diseased patient, and the science.

The Pathology Undergraduate Curriculum 2019 Second Edition describes what should be taught today. To know how to complete a death certificate; to know the stages of death, etc. Pathology teaching has been integrated into other disciplines. There is increased use of computer-assisted learning and high-quality textbooks. Certainly, histology learning is of high quality on internet sites. I suppose today's teaching is more practical for the jobs the students will take up. However, that is not necessarily what university teaching is all about.

Oh dear! One is not allowed to harp back to the good old days!

I have written about seventeen professors in this chapter. A significant number I regard as friends, as you will have read. The last four were highly respected by me. However, none of these were friends. I only met once Prof. Blandy, one to one regarding the kidney work. He was friendly but not a friend. He did tick me off when I was a house officer. I had forgotten to tell him that a patient had died a day after he had operated. He came on a ward round, opened the door of the single room was confronted by the patient lying on the bed wrapped in a shroud.

I have shown that professors can embody qualities such as being fun, inspiring, and motivating. These qualities are positive additions when developing a friendship with a professor. My friendships, whatever depth, have brought about an enriching experience. That is not to say that I do not have enriching experiences with others of my friends.

CHAPTER 3

Cruising along

In 1934 my mother and her mother, Lily, went cruising to Cuba on the *SS Oriente*. This boat was part of the Ward line. The Ward line had ships sailing regularly to Cuba since the middle of the nineteenth century. The *Oriente* was built in 1930 along with its sister cruise ship, the *SS Morro Castle*. On 8 September that year (1934), the *Morro Castle* caught fire and 137 of the passengers and crew died. My mother and grandmother could easily have been on that ship.

SS Oriente

I have the original menu for the farewell dinner of my mother's cruise.

Farewell Dinner Menu, Cuba Cruise, 1934. *SS Oriente*

I would choose caviar, consommé, sole, duckling and apple pie.

Frank Sloan was my half-brother, my father's son from his first marriage. He was ten years older than me, and he joined the merchant Navy when he was in his late teens. His first voyage was on a small cargo ship. The voyage took eighteen months without returning to the UK. My father bought a small globe so he could see where Frank was. Frank started courses that led towards his becoming a radio officer. We did not live in the same home for long and I think I only went on holiday with Frank and my parents once. He did stay at our home when he was on leave. I idolised him when I was a teenager. When he was learning Morse code, I wrote him notes in Morse and delivered them under his bedroom door. Eventually he became a radio officer and progressed to senior radio officer grade. He started working on cruise ships and his last ship was the *Canberra*. He grew to dislike working on cruise ships and he and his wife, Florence, went together on an oil tanker which went up and down the Red Sea for many weeks at a time. They were pleased that smoking was allowed in their quarters on the tanker! He retired from the merchant navy on ill health grounds. He obtained an external BA in History in 1994.

Frank Sloan at BA degree ceremony

My parents became interested in cruising holidays because of Frank. At one point, we went on a cruise every two years with the interim year's holiday taken in Germany. The cruises were on ships of the P&O (the Peninsular and Oriental Steam Navigation Company).

As a youngster and a young teenager, I had a whale of a time on cruises and usually made friends with those of my age group. I also loved the company of older people. They had some fascinating stories to tell. So now I am an older person telling the stories! We sat with the same people in the dining room in the evenings and got to know them well. On one cruise, we were amazed that a 90-year-old man went swimming every day. That was in the 1950s. Age and activity is hardly regarded as remarkable these days. On one cruise, there was a man on our table called Mr. Lesser. I was always sworn to secrecy by my parents not to tell anybody they were doctors. It emerged that Mr. Lesser worked for the General Medical Council (GMC), responsible for striking doctors off the register. I think my parents confessed to Mr. Lesser that they were general medical practitioners in the middle of the cruise. It would have been wrong not to have done so.

I think the first cruise I went on was with the orient liner *SS Orcades*. We also holidayed on the *SS Orsova*. We always travelled first class. The separation of first and second class was strict. I found out that, on one cruise, a friend of mine from school was with his parents and that they were travelling second class. I was allowed to visit him, but he was not allowed to come to the first-class areas. I had to obtain written permission for the visit.

Below are three photographs of the *Orcades* (from ssmaritime.com, accessed 1 3 22).

The *Orcades* in 1952

Children's play area

The ballroom

Some memories of the cruises with my parents stand out for me. On the 29 May 1953 Hillary and Tenzing reached the summit of Mount Everest. Four days later, on the 2 June, it was the coronation of Queen Elizabeth II. We were on a cruise in the Mediterranean. There was excitement at the announcement of both of those events on the boat. We therefore did not have the experience like many others back home of crowding round televisions to watch the coronation. However, a lengthy news reel got to the ship somehow and we watched the film of both the events. I was about 7 ½ years old.

Another cruise was in 1956 and again in the Mediterranean. There was an announcement that an Egyptian gunboat was approaching us. The captain reassured us that we were safe because none of the shells on the Egyptian boat fitted the guns. I seem to remember things about the boats rather than any of the ports as the former was where the fun took place.

Later, when I was a young teenager, we went on a transatlantic cruise which called at Bermuda and New York. One evening on the way to Bermuda and a long way across the Atlantic, we had fog and the fog alarms were sounding. It was an eerie sound in those days and often with an echo. We were enjoying our dinner at the time. The waiter looked at me and said, "I thought you might be interested that this is the exact spot where the Titanic sank." That resulted in my being a bit frightened. I am sure they do that all the time wherever the fog comes down.

After docking in Bermuda, we went on an excursion round part of the coast on a small motorboat. I think there were about thirty people on board. Lunch was served, but the thing I remember most was a drink called a rum swizzle. A Bermuda rum swizzle is the national drink. The original swizzle stick was snapped off a tree. Recipes vary but the main ingredients are rum, orange and pineapple juice. The final ingredient on this excursion was brought to the mixture by the captain of the boat. It was a very small measure of engine oil!

New York was the next stop and one of the highlights was the approach to New York at sunrise and cruising past the Statue of

Liberty. We all got up very early and I was the proud possessor of a 35 mm camera. I took thirty-six photographs of that sunrise approach to the city with its unique skyline. I think we were there for two nights and there were daytime excursions. Our ship docked very close to the original *RMS Queen Elizabeth*. It seemed massive to me, and I took a photograph of the bows standing directly in front.

RMS Queen Elizabeth. Bows.
Docked in New York Harbour, 1945
Getty images.co.au

On one of the evenings in New York, my parents went out to the city on an excursion, and I was left on the boat. I was quite happy being looked after on the boat as I had made friends with other young people. I did not realise for a few days that they had been to a nightclub. The club was in the Bowery, the oldest area of New York. The outing was accompanied by the ship's photographer and the next day photographs were displayed on boards for purchase. There was one of my father poking his head from behind a plump woman's rear. She was obviously one of the dance performers. I was slightly shocked. I had an image of my father as a teetotaller saint. My mother sometimes labelled themselves as "the saint and the sinner". My mother had been a bit of a raver in her youth and liked a drink!

The last boat trip I did with my parents was from Leningrad to Southampton on a Russian ship. Indeed, it was the last holiday I took with them. I had just started university and I thought holidaying with my parents had already finished. However, I could not resist my father's temptation: "How would you like to go to Russia, son?" It was a bus trip from London via Berlin, Warsaw, Omsk, Smolensk, and Moscow. (I danced the twist in Moscow with a young English woman who was on the tour). Then we took a train to Leningrad, as it was called then (its name was changed back to Saint Petersburg in 1991). The Russian ship took us from Leningrad to Southampton. Every member of the crew was Russian. It was not a huge ship and was very pleasant. The crossing was smooth. I have only two memories of that voyage. My parents had gone to bed, and I was having a drink at the bar. I got chatting to a man about various things and asked him what he thought about the Russians. He replied but he was one of the ship's officers, the purser, and was Russian. He spoke in immaculate English. The other memory was of an entertainment evening when the crew came out and played balalaikas and sang in fantastic harmony both Russian and British songs.

I have always been in the habit of saying that my last experience was the best experience I have ever had. The last film was the best film I had ever seen; the last book was the best book I had ever read. The next cruise I will describe will buck this trend. It was a Caribbean cruise with Felicity, my first wife, on the *QE2* in February 1976. It was a great cruise and was the best so far. I would like to thank Felicity Davies, my first wife, for filling in my memory gaps with some comments on this section.

The *QE2* in 2008

The holiday started with us flying to New York, where we embarked. After we were relieved of our luggage, we entered the boat on one of the lower decks. There was a man playing an upright piano and we were pretty sure we recognised him. It was Victor Borge. We discovered soon afterwards that he was the main act of the entertainment.

Felicity and I lived in Cheltenham, and she was a friend of the person who managed the labour ward in the maternity unit, Pat Connerty. Her husband, Chris, was a radio officer on the *QE2*. Chris was working on the ship when we went on this cruise and Pat was a passenger.

First and second class had disappeared from most cruise ships by that time. However, on the *QE2* there were three different dining rooms: in descending order of poshness, the Queen's Grill, the Princess Grill, and the Columbia Grill. How much you spent on your cabin determined which restaurant you were allocated to. We were lucky that Chris Connerty upgraded us from the Columbia to the Princess Grill. We were seated in an area where some of the cruise lecturers and performers sat. (I think Victor Borge ate elsewhere!) The menu was superb. I was under the impression that the Queen's Grill (which seated about one hundred) had no menu and one could ask for anything. Researching on the internet I found that there was indeed a menu in the Queen's Grill. It was the same throughout the three restaurants. However, in the Queen's Grill one could also ask for anything. We heard that one table asked for fish and chips wrapped in the *News of the World*. They got it!

The first scheduled stop was Bermuda. We were having breakfast and it was a bit rough. A force-nine gale! The captain came on the tannoy system and announced that we could not dock in Bermuda because of the weather. People clapped after the announcement because we were all enjoying the ship so much. We headed for the Caribbean and the weather calmed. We visited Barbados, Trinidad, Martinique, St. Thomas, Curaçao and Caracas. Pat Connerty knew Barbados because she had worked there and showed us the sights. When we disembarked at Trinidad, we did not like it and felt threatened walking along the dock from the ship. We turned round and went back on the ship. That is the shortest time I have been in another country (Trinidad became a self-governing independent nation in 1962). The second shortest was Laos – 30 minutes!

Trinidad is just short of 7 miles from Venezuela. The next stop was Caracas. This was my first and only visit to a South American country. We left the boat in a tour bus and saw the hundreds of shacks on a hill, where the poorest of the poor lived. At that time the poverty situation in Venezuela was awful and it has got worse in recent years. The slums are called barrios.

Barrios, Venezuela

We were taken on to a great contrast with this abject poverty. I think it was the Caracas Country Club, where there is a dress code for members.

"It may seem remarkable, if not obscene, that a citadel like this exists, and thrives, in the middle of one of the world's most violent and distressed cities, the capital of a country whose economy has collapsed and where malnutrition and disease rates are soaring. Millions have emigrated to escape the grind of finding enough to eat, of living without reliable electricity or tap water. And here, inside a gracious hacienda where chandeliers twinkle overhead, there is renewed focus on sartorial protocol." Bloomberg.com, accessed 9/3/22.

In the afternoon we went to La Rinconada Hippodrome, the Caracas racecourse. I even had a wager and won.

I will now digress. The ship's cinema and theatre were designed by a cousin of my mother's, Gaby Schreiber. Her maiden name was Wolff and she was born in Berlin. My mother told me that Gaby was ashamed of being German and told everyone she was born in Austria. Searching for her recently on the internet confirmed this Austria tale. Klaus Turner (Wolff) and his sister, Brigitte Wolff, who was single, lived in adjacent apartments in Kensington. I saw them quite a lot when I was a student. Klaus worked in the Burberry shop in Regent Street. Brigitte was a histology scientist working on breast cancer with Sir Hedley Atkins, who became the president of the Royal College of Surgeons. When Klaus and Brigitte retired, they moved to the outskirts of London and lived in adjacent cottages somewhere in the countryside. I visited them once with my mother. Gaby was staying, and when we arrived, she was resting in a bedroom. She did not come out for ages, allegedly because she wanted to make sure she looked her best! We were not posh enough really. She lived in a flat in Eaton Square in London, one of the most fashionable squares inhabited by the very rich.

Gaby Schreiber, University   Cinema/theatre *QE2*
of Brighton blog

Victor Borge did not perform in the theatre. Despite it having 491 seats, it was not big enough. Everyone wanted to see him. Seats were brought into a very large area of the ship. He did two performances. He was very funny, as usual. Some of his best stuff was about the ship and the captain. Of course, he played the piano in his usual style. If you have never seen him, search for him on YouTube.

There was a talk in the theatre by Isaac Asimov, the science fiction writer. I went to that myself and enjoyed it. We also watched the film "Jaws" in the cinema/theatre. They always put a crew member on the door who only had one arm. It was the days when there was no significant recycling of food waste on ships. I think 2 tons of food waste was thrown overboard every day. We were told that the ship was constantly followed by hungry sharks.

Victor Borge

The *QE2* cruise was the last I did until after Kath died in February 2015. Kath was a very poor sailor and suffered from motion sickness, including in cars. I have close friends who live in Pontefract, about 4 miles from me. Jennifer Doncaster lived in the house next door here in Castleford when we were 9 years old. I, her family and various other friends have been together on eight cruises since then. The first was a P&O cruise and the remaining seven, Fred Olsen. I will describe each cruise using a title, two photographs and one or two sentences of comments.

1. Jul/Aug 2015. P&O – *Azura*. Norwegian fjords.

A glacier   The *Azura*

We all felt the ship was far too large with 3000 passengers, but the scenery was stunning.

2. Dec 2015. Fred Olsen – *Boudicca*. Bruges and Amsterdam.

Bruges   Chocolate

Beautiful Bruges was full of chocolate but pleasantly empty of tourists for our visit.

3. Aug 2016. Fred Olsen – *Black Watch*. Faroe Islands and Iceland.

Our ship   Alan Franks

My good friend Alan fell in love with the Faroe Islands. He tragically died shortly after this, his first cruise.

4. Sept/Oct 2016. Fred Olsen – *Balmoral*. Corunna, Porto. Lisbon.

A Henry Moore statue in Porto   Lisbon

My relations, Martin and Jen, loved this cruise to such an extent that they revisited some of the places the following year. They particularly liked Porto, as did I.

5. 20 Dec 2016. Fred Olsen – *Black Watch*. German Christmas Markets. Hamburg.

Christmas at Hamburg

The day before our visit a truck deliberately ran into the Hamburg Christmas market and twelve people were killed with fifty-six injured. As an act of defiance from the Hamburg people, the market was packed and buzzing the next late afternoon.

6. Feb/Mar 2017. Fred Olsen – *Braemar*. Caribbean.

St. Lucia coast   Atlantic Ocean

The flora and scenery on the islands were stunning. We returned to the UK with an Atlantic crossing taking six days. I enjoyed seeing only the sea for days on end. Not even a bird. It was a smooth crossing. Not everyone likes that. I love the sea.

7. Aug 2017. Fred Olsen – *Balmoral*. Norwegian Fjords.

Kath Overton and mountain goat   Bergen

The trip up Mount Fløyen on a funicular railway for an expensive lunch and seeing the goats was a treat. One goat was called Obama and another, Elvis.

8. Nov 2018. Fred Olsen – *Braemar*. River Seine.

The Seine   Honfleur

A very relaxing short cruise. The port of Honfleur was a delightful place to explore on foot.

This was the last cruise I have been on.

I always enjoy the interesting lectures and talks by people brought in by the cruise company. I got the crazy idea that I could do these and get myself a free cruise! I enjoy making PowerPoint presentations. On one of the Fred Olsen cruises there was a retired policeman,

Bob Dixon, who gave a couple of talks on being a "Bobby on the Beat". He was a policeman in the East End of London in the 1960s. I was a medical student and then worked in the East End at the same time. I befriended him over a cup of coffee one morning. He explained that one had to get an agent. It was fortunate that the agent worked from Yorkshire. When I got home, I prepared two talks. The first was about my early life at home and then as a medical student. The second was about general practice. The talks were to be no more than 45 minutes long, as someone might be speaking/entertaining after me. I practiced one of the talks with a group of local people I got together and supplied with a buffet lunch. I asked for honest feedback. I received some valuable and constructive comments. Comments could be made anonymously.

I have been running a group for retired GPs for over a decade. One of my fellow retired GPs asked a friend of his to give us a talk. It was about his voluntary dental work in Africa. I found it fascinating. While I was chatting to him, I said he ought to do that talk on cruise ships. He told me that the agent had turned him down. When I heard that, I gave up on this daydream of a project! However, I have given these talks a few times to different audiences and they apparently went down well.

I have had a long-standing ambition to do a transatlantic crossing on the *Queen Mary 2*.

I nearly booked a trip in 2021. It was a "literature festival" cruise. There were famous writers giving the talks. One was Simon Armitage and another, Pam Ayres (I last heard her give a talk in the mid-1970s in the Queens Hotel in Cheltenham). It was a daydream I chickened out from. I would be on my own (that is OK these days), but I think I would be out of my depth with my fellow intellectual and well-read passengers. As a fully certified ignoramus, I would have to be bluffing and bullshitting most of the time!

Cruising is an attractive way of holidaying for the very young and the elderly, especially if one departs from the land where one lives. It is so much easier than battling the queues at an airport.

When I was at school and the hymn was "Eternal Father Strong to Save (For those in peril on the sea)", I always thought of my half-brother, Frank. When I hear it now, it brings tears to my eyes, and I think of Frank. On 3 April 2022, I watched the Pope live on YouTube. He was visiting Malta. While the 20,000 people waited for him to arrive to celebrate Mass, that hymn was played. The reason was partly because the Apostle Paul arrived as a refugee to that island on a boat and was welcomed with open arms. Malta has also accepted refugees arriving by boat in recent times.

In mid-November 2022, I did go on a transatlantic crossing from Southampton to New York on Cunard's *Queen Mary 2*.

The *Queen Mary 2*

The ship (I got told off for calling it a boat) is magnificent. It not a cruise ship although it does sail for cruises. It was designed to deal with Atlantic seas. There is a video on YouTube entitled "QM2 vs QE2" (https://youtu.be/AFgq-Pao8h8), which of course interested me, now having sailed on each.

I travelled with Steve and Jane. Jane was a goddaughter of my late wife, Kath, and I have unilaterally (unofficially) adopted her as my goddaughter. I have known them both for decades. Jane is the daughter of two of our, now my, closest friends, Kath and Alan. It was the trip of a lifetime for all of us.

Jane and me, *QM2*

Cruising is near perfect for a lot of older and single older people like me. I hope to travel on more cruises.

CHAPTER 4

Cultivating friendship in the garden

I became more and more interested in the garden as the pandemic progressed in 2020. I have always taken photographs of the progress of the plants, shrubs, and trees. This chapter shows what a wealth of colour and growth there is in my garden. The garden has evolved since about 1922. The major influences on this garden have been my father and his first wife, then my parents and finally my late wife, Kath. The garden was certainly my friend during the pandemic lockdown when we were not allowed to mix with friends properly.

I have taken photographs since the lockdown in March 2020. Below are photographs from that date to February 2021. I have chosen two photographs from each month. However, before that is a little history of the garden and photographs of its layout.

Tieve Tara in about 1924

The house was built for my father. He was the doctor for Fryston Colliery, which was owned privately. The house was bought by the colliery and rented to my father. He bought it a couple of years later.

Front garden in 1969 showing the ivy and veranda

The house is surrounded by garden areas on three sides. The fourth side of the house is semi-detached from the medical centre. Here follows photos that show the layout of the garden. Tieve Tara was renamed Hill House in 2006.

Hill House kitchen patio and study garden

Side garden, view from garage

Side garden, view from front garden

Front garden, view from gate

Front garden, view from Medical Centre extension

Front garden, view from conservatory

My parents were never without a gardener, and when the time of year was right, had a local company visit and plant bedding, plants and more. The gardeners were generally patients. Mr. Siddens, who had Parkinson's disease, was the gardener when I was about 4 years old. He used to pat me on my head, and I could feel his hand shaking. Ronnie had a severe and enduring mental health problem and became my patient when I came back to Airedale. Eric was my mother's gardener when she lived in this house, and when she retired to a bungalow. Eric's partner was Mrs. Platt, and she had had a stroke. Nevertheless, she managed to do a bit of painting and decorating in our house. My mother was very interested in the garden and had a small vegetable patch at one point. One could get out of the wind and rain and shelter in the veranda and enjoy seeing the main blooms in the garden, which were across the lawn. So, the garden has many memories of my youth. It was a children's friend with a swing, and a hidden area where I could dig a deep hole and start tunneling to my friend, Graham Greatbatch, who lived a mile away.

My father enjoyed cutting the lawn with a petrol engine lawnmower. I inherited that from him and eventually moved from petrol to an electric mower. Kath was the main person who managed the evolution of the garden. She asked me to take photographs at certain times of the year so that she could see where blooms were required the following year. She did some quite heavy work in the garden, and I could see her out of my consulting room window when I was working. I have never been interested in working in the garden. Perhaps that is because I am lazy.

When we got older, we did employ gardeners and after Kath died. I certainly needed a gardener. However, there were no gardeners coming for a long time during the Covid lockdown. This is the time my friendship with the garden progressed. I had to clear the dust and cobwebs from the electric mower and find some gardening tools. I tried to do 10 minutes' gardening, no more, no less, every day. I've got to know the various and many plants and shrubs better and become interested in their lives.

There are three places where one can sit in the garden. There is also a water feature, which I can turn on and off with my mobile phone. Many birds came, and I loved photographing them, particularly the woodpecker. However, I have had to stop feeding birds because the feeders attract rats. The veranda was replaced by a conservatory, and it is a lovely place to sit in the winter and enjoy the garden covered in snow. I spend a lot of time in my study, and this has patio doors that open into a part of the garden which has artificial grass. The water feature is there. There are some beautiful rose bushes. There is a garden seat for two and a coffee table there. The house is surrounded by powerful spotlights. There are two patios, each with a table and chairs. There is a remote-controlled awning that is large and covers of significant area of the larger patio outside the kitchen. During Covid, I had the neighbours round for a drink and we sat outside to obey the rules. There was a powerful thunderstorm, but we did not move and were kept quite dry. The garden is surrounded by tall trees, which makes it private.

The garden is not only a close friend, but also a quiet sanctuary. When I have been away and return to open the gates, the garden welcomes me. Like the politician, the late Roy Jenkins, I often do my daily walking round the garden and check my friend is happy. I could easily have included another fifty photographs for this chapter.

March 2020

Chinese magnolia

Hanging forsythia

April 2020

Lenten rose

Flowering apple

May 2020

Northern iris

Common lilac

June 2020

Pink-sorrel

Bigleaf hydrangea

July 2020

Poet's jasmine

Honeysuckle

August 2020

Tall Oregon grape

China Rose (David Austin)

September 2020

Uruguayan pampas grass

Fuchsia

October 2020

Highbush blueberry

Smoke tree

November 2020

English holly

Silver birch

December 2020

Winter creeper

Majorcan hellebore

January 2021

Japanese meadowsweet

Snowdrop

February 2021

Early ladybird on flowering currant

American holly

The kitchen garden at night

I have an application on my iPhone called "PictureThis". At the time of writing, it costs £19 a year. The application has a camera facility. A photograph can be taken of a plant, flower, tree shrub, etc. The application will then provide information about the name and other details of that particular flora. I was totally ignorant about the names of plants, and this has helped me label the lovely growth in my garden. On the following page is a list of the various flora I have identified in 2021. In June 2023 I identified more.

Wintergreen barberry	China rose
Swiss Stone pine	Oregon grape
Common foxglove	Pampas grass
Cabbage tree	Lingonberry
Majorcan hellebore	Highbush blueberry
Red flowering currant	Smoke tree
English ivy	Common holly
Common jasmine	Wintercreeper
European honeysuckle	Japanese meadowsweet

American holly
Bigleaf hydrangea
Lenten rose
Tulip
Wood forget-me-not
Daffodil
Bigleaf periwinkle
Rosemary
Common hyacinth
Bay laurel
Bukhara fleeceflower
Armenian grape hyacinth
Sweet violet
Pink-sorrel
Common boxwood
Common barberry
Anemone clematis
Northern blue flag Iris
Asiatic apple
Bigleaf periwinkle
Common periwinkle
Yaupon
Judas tree
Saucer magnolia
Weeping forsythia
Heartleaf Bergenia
Japanese white pine
Great false leopard's bane
Pansy
California privet
Evergreen spindle
Adam's needle
Silver birch
Twinberry honeysuckle
Common sheep sorrel
Bluebell
Black cottonwood
Plantain lily

Green hellebore
Rockspray cotoneaster
Laurustinus
Smooth hydrangea
Wild meadowsweet
Blastus cochinchinensis
Ground elder
Blueblossom
Bridal veil broom
Round-headed leek
Virginia creeper
Japanese barberry
Mountain clematis
Lilac
Rhododendron maximum
Germander speedwell
Evergreen huckleberry
Pink rock-rose
Mexican orange (Choisya)
Willow-leaved cotoneaster
Red osier dogwood
White meadowsweet
Spanish bluebell
Wood spurge
Garlic mustard
Common dandelion
Common daisy
Bearded iris
Shrubby cinquefoil
Common peony
Korean rose
Pinks
Cape marguerite
Beach aster
Lemon balm
Pale smartweed
Tutsan
Orange lily

Fringed willowherb
Orange daylily
Lewis' mock-orange
English lavender
Fuchsia
European blackberry
Tea rose
Hemp agrimony
Bearberry cotoneaster
Mentigi
Peach-leaved bellflower
Chinese privet
Cretan bryony
Austrian brier
Garden snapdragon
Butterfly bush
Big blue lilyturf

Wheat
Grape leaf anemone
Garden cosmos
Rose of Sharon
Japanese honeysuckle

New June 2023

Small scabious
Siskiyou lewisia
Dog rose
Elmleaf blackberry
Veronica rakaiensis
Garden petunia
Bacopa
Wall bellflower
Common columbine

CHAPTER 5

Following the science

Science is not just a collection of knowledge. It is a lifelong friend who is with you on a road to discovery. This friend guides you to turn the unknown into the known. Science celebrates with you when you make a discovery. You will see that science has been my friend for over half a century and will remain so for the rest of my life. This chapter describes my personal experience of science as well as my thoughts and reflections.

During the pandemic that started in 2020 the phrase "following the science" was repeated incessantly by politicians. The approach of scientists worldwide has been exemplary and as honest as is possible. In April 2021, I tested myself for coronavirus using a kit (the lateral flow test). I ordered seven kits from the government website, which I received in the post two days later. A week before that I received my second Pfizer vaccination against Covid (coronavirus disease). I had a booster vaccination in mid-October 2021 and later that month tested positive for and had Covid. I tested positive again for Covid at the end of March 2022 and my fourth Spring booster was due about then. It was delayed four weeks in accordance with the guidelines.

The coronavirus was identified first at the start of January 2020. The first vaccination was given in the UK on 8 December 2020 to a 90-year-old woman. The vaccination was developed in the UK. Development of vaccinations can take many years and sometimes cannot be developed at all depending on the disease. I marvel at the speed and accuracy of the science involved with all this.

I have thought a lot about science since the pandemic started. I have had a deep interest in science since the 1970s, when I was involved in scientific research full time for about four and a half years: an undergraduate degree and then a research post as a lecturer in physiology at the London Hospital Medical College, University of London. I feel I am a scientist for life, even though my formal scientific career ended many decades ago. This is not a conclusion with an objective to boost my ego or show off. I question things, search the literature for evidence and correspond occasionally with fellow scientists about aspects of human temperature regulation.

The time I became intimately involved with science started with eighteen months taken out of my undergraduate medical training, to undertake a research degree in Anatomy. The Merriam-Webster dictionary gives several definitions of anatomy. I favour "the structural makeup especially of an organism or any of its parts". For example, human anatomy; the anatomy of birds; the anatomy of the ape's skull. Anatomy is also "a separating or dividing into parts for detailed examination", e.g. a human body, but also "the anatomy of a marriage". As a GP it is useful to know where parts of the body are, relating to an adult, a developing baby, child and during a woman's pregnancy.

At the London Hospital Medical College, I undertook research on human temperature regulation in the department of physiology. Physiology is the science of life, and research in physiology helps us to understand how the body works. If one understands how the human body works under normal conditions, then it must be easier to understand what is going wrong in a patient with symptoms.

There are many similar definitions of science. One that I like is:

> "Science is the pursuit of knowledge and understanding of the natural and social world following a systematic methodology based on evidence." The Science Council, 2009.

> "Because 'science' denotes such a very wide range of activities a definition of it needs to be general; it certainly needs to cover investigation of the social as well as natural worlds; it needs the words "systematic" and "evidence"; and it needs to be simple and short. The definition succeeds in all these respects admirably, and I applaud it therefore." The philosopher AC Grayling. *The Guardian*, 2009.

I joined a fantastic group of scientists working in the physiology department when I started there at the end of 1970. The head of department was Professor Kenneth Cross and the relatively recently appointed reader was Dr. W.R Keatinge (Bill). (See chapter 2) Bill met me and showed me where I would be working and introduced me to the academic and technical staff. He suggested I spent three months settling in and seeing what research was being undertaken. I could then decide with whom I wanted to work with, and that person would be my PhD supervisor.

Professor W. R. (Bill) Keatinge

There was a broad spectrum of research being undertaken. I have described my then colleagues and their work in a previous publication (*The English Doctor*, 2012). I decided I did not wish to do research on animals but rather human research. Bill Keatinge was working with Jeff Graham on the physiology of the nerve supply to the muscles of sheep arteries. Jeff befriended me. Some others of the academic staff had told me how awkward Bill could be. However, what Jeff told me about Bill made me choose him to be my supervisor. I never regretted that and am pleased that I remained in contact with him over the years until his death. I have met Jeff and his wife, Sylvia, in recent years. What a luxury to be able to choose with whom one worked.

I would like to quote from a full-page obituary of Bill published in the *British Medical Journal* in August 2008 written by Caroline Richmond.

"His failures included failing to resuscitate a polar bear with a broken neck. He was in Alaska attempting to study temperature before, during, and after hibernation in a pair of bears. The bears had been shot with short acting anaesthetic darts. One was knocked out as intended but the other ran into, and up, a tree, falling off. While Bill was attempting to resuscitate it, he was unaware it had broken its neck. His colleagues inserted a rectal probe in the other bear which woke up, very aggrieved. Exit Keatinge, pursued by a bear."

Bill was an amazing supervisor for my PhD research. I worked for him for three years. We met at least once a fortnight to discuss my work. I could ask him anything. He was a very kind man. I felt that the work was truly a joint effort, and I totally respected his experience in experimental design as well as writing up the work. He allowed me to develop ideas and branch off down areas of interest. This resulted in my PhD reporting about three areas of our research.

1. The effect of local temperature changes at the head on sublingual and oesophageal temperatures.
2. The measurement of deep body temperature from external auditory canal with servo-controlled heating around ear.
3. The role of body size, sex and subcutaneous fat in cooling young people swimming in cold water.

The idea of doing the third area of research developed from past work by Bill and other colleagues on the cooling of adults in cold water. Nothing much had then been done to study young people and children swimming in cold water.

A large part of the work was taken up on the most suitable methods for the planned studies. Measurement should not be affected by local factors and should reflect, rapidly and quantitatively, changes in temperature. The body temperature of arterial blood at the centre of the body near the heart estimates deep body temperature (core temperature). It is this temperature that the body tries to keep within a narrow range to prevent fever or hypothermia. Oesophageal (food pipe) temperature measured at heart level parallels rapid changes in aortic blood temperature closely. This temperature was, therefore, the most informative measure of deep body temperature and is the site we used, despite some volunteers experiencing discomfort with the insertion of the thermometer and lead down the food pipe.

The only estimate of body temperature I was familiar with was sublingual measurement using a portable mercury-in-glass thermometer. I wondered how accurate these were, and that was the start of the research. Sublingual digital thermometers were also available.

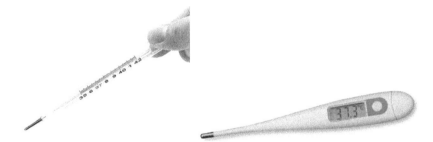

Glass sublingual thermometer   Digital electronic sublingual thermometer

Many of the readers of this essay will be familiar with the thermometer I have just described, and so I want to describe in detail the experiments I did to determine the accuracy of measuring body temperature using the site under the tongue (sublingual).

Volunteers for the sublingual temperature experiment were medical students, nurses and physiologists working in the London Hospital Medical College. I never did any experiments that I had not done on myself first, apart from those involved in the swimming children project.

Next to my laboratory was a temperature-controlled room, which was used in all experiments apart from the one on children. The air temperature near the subject could be maintained within 0.5°C of any temperature from 0 to 46°C. The room was fitted with thermostatic control heating and refrigeration units. Essentials controlling these units were suspended in the centre of the room.

Using additional heaters, the air temperature of this room could be increased from 10 to 40°C in less than 40 minutes. The net wind speed near the subject was 0.3 to 0.7 m/s. The extra fans, heaters, water baths and chairs were in standard positions for all experiments. Recording instruments were in an adjacent room. Leads from a subject could be fed through a hole in the door between the rooms. The temperature of the instrument room did not change more than 0.5°C during any experiment. Heating or cooling thermometer leads to temperatures between 0 and 46° within 4 cm of the sensor did not alter its reading of a constant temperature bath, indicating negative or stem conduction errors.

Thermometers were calibrated before and after each experiment against a 0 to 40° mercury-in-glass thermometer (British Standard 593/54), which gave readings to + or – 0.05°C. A rapidly stirred thermostatically controlled water bath (Shannon, London) was used for calibrations maintained at a temperature of 25 to 45°C, + or – 0.025°C.

Readers who might have glazed over nor nodded off at this point will be pleased to know I will be not going into many more details of instrumentation! I just wanted to demonstrate how careful we were with everything to try and make sure results were true. Before doing experiments, a common question would be "But what if...?" But what if a change in temperature of the leads from the instrument affects the readings? But what if the subjects experienced different dietary intakes before the experiment? But what if the saliva cools down and affects the mouth temperature?

Of course, I could not resist some basic experiments on myself before the proper study was planned. I took my sublingual temperature in my nice warm laboratory, spent 10 minutes in the cold room and took it again. It had gone down by nearly 1°C.

Sublingual and oesophageal temperatures were measured in forty experiments on fourteen volunteers, seven male and seven female. Readings were made every 2 minutes for 30 minutes at room temperature and then for a further 30 minutes in colder or warmer air temperatures between 3.5 to 45°C. On eleven occasions the subject then returned to the warmer room at 17 to 24.5°C for a further 20 minutes. The head was uncovered, and long hair tied back.

Below are the results from two different individuals shown as graphs.

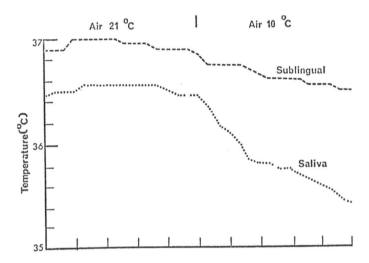

The effects of warm air on sublingual temperature on one person

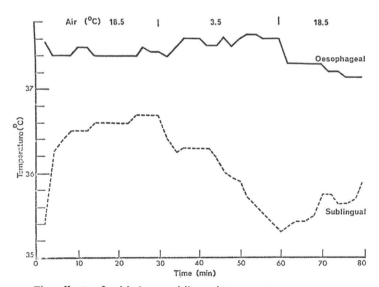

The effects of cold air on sublingual temperature on one person

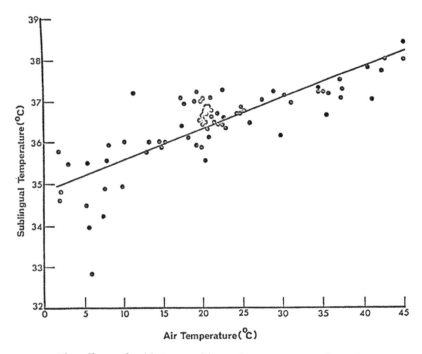

The effects of cold air on sublingual temperature, all results

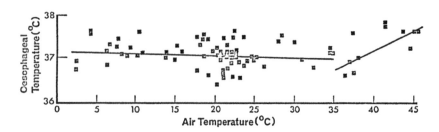

The effects of cold air on oesophageal temperature, all results.
Insulation of the head and neck prevented cooling to a large extent

But what is the effect of breathing cold air and cooling of the skin on sublingual temperatures?

Six volunteers from the first series of experiments repeated a 30-minute exposure to air in the warm and then 30 minutes in the cold at 3.5 to 10°C. The head and neck were insulated with a thick layer of cotton wool with small holes to expose the eyes and mouth. After 30 minutes, insulation was removed from some subjects in the cold room and readings continued. Cold exposures were made by two volunteers with permanent tracheostomies. It was assumed that, as in the earlier experiments, oesophageal temperature did not change. It was not measured so as not to cause any discomfort to these patients. In these two volunteers, breathing was not through the mouth but through the neck by means of a tracheostomy.

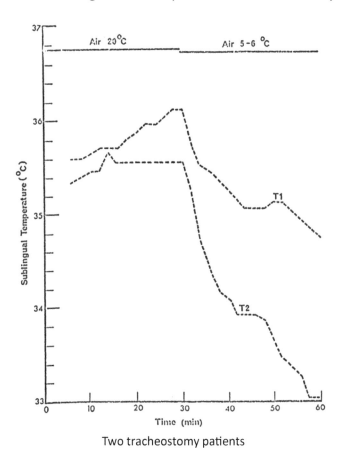

Two tracheostomy patients

So, it was not to do with breathing. What was the role of saliva?

We took advice from Ron Spiers, the reader in dental physiology. He showed me how to attach a gadget called a Lashley cannula to the inside of the cheek, so it collected the saliva from the outlet of the parotid salivary gland duct. The cannula was altered so it had a thermistor to measure the temperature of the saliva as it came out of the duct. So, the flow rate and the temperature of the saliva could be measured when the subject was exposed to cold air.

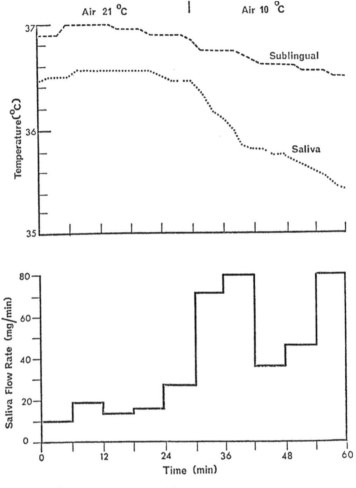

Saliva temperature and flow rate in one of the six
subjects exposed to cold air

There was a lot more information discovered about the errors in sublingual temperature measurement that could result in under-reading and therefore possibly missing a fever.

On reflection, I estimate that the work on sublingual temperature was about a quarter of the research undertaken in those three years.

It involves a huge amount of reading and quoting evidence from the past. For example, at one point I got very excited to think that we were the first researchers to think that saliva could affect sublingual temperature. I searched high and low for a reference from the past and failed. I used the Royal Society of Medicine (RSM) Library. Ron Spiers got me in to the dental library. Then, blow me, I found a reference in the basement of the RSM: Dorodnitsina, A. A, (1937) The influence of cooling and heating on the unconditioned salivary reflexes in man. *Fiz. Zhur SSSR*, 23, (1), 111–116. This was the only work on the effects of a short exposure of the head to cold on saliva. I think the head was inserted into a fridge with the door open!

Our work was published in the *British Medical Journal* in 1975. It has been cited (quoted) 23 times since it was published, the last time being in 2021 in an article published in the *American Journal of Physiology*. One significant thing for me is that I have not come across a publication that refutes the work. It is a warm feeling that one's research published almost fifty years ago is still recognised.

The second piece of work took well over a year to plan, execute, and study the readings. It resulted in the invention of an electronic thermometer, which Bill called the Zero Gradient Aural Thermometer (ZGAT). It measured the temperature with a thermojunction in the auditory canal of the ear. It had a servo-controlled heating pad covering the ear. This resulted in the temperature of the pad remaining the same as that of the auditory canal. The results indicated that aural temperature measured by the ZGAT closely parallels rapid changes in oesophageal temperature with no local cooling under these conditions. The lowest environmental temperature recommended for this is 9°C. Initial readings were made with a prototype built in the department of physiology by the senior electronics technician, Tony Barnett. He was an amazing person and very skilled indeed. I did a little bit of soldering! The prototype was approximately 4 feet 6 inches tall, 3 feet wide and 1 foot deep. I wish I had a photograph of Tony and the prototype. We worked with a medical instruments company called Addison Process Control Ltd. (a subsidiary of Muirhead Ltd.), and the machine was manufactured and sold.

One of the instruments is kept in the National Collection Centre of the Science Museum, where objects are stored. These are being gradually digitised to the online collection. The photographs below are from that website. The building for these objects is being constructed and will open to the public in 2024. If I am still here, I would love to visit.

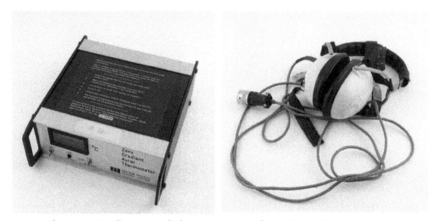

The Zero Gradient Aural Thermometer – from the online collection of the National Collection Centre, UK Science Museum. Machine donated by St. Pancras Hospital

The work was published in the Proceedings of the Physiological Society in 1973 and the *Journal of Applied Physiology* in 1975. The first paper has had 17 citations. The more detailed second paper has been cited 69 times, 6 since 2018.

To have a paper published by the Physiological Society, I had to do a demonstration at one of their conferences which took place in Oxford. The demonstration involved one of the senior technicians, Adrian Jacobs, sitting in his swimming trunks with his legs being cooled in a tank of temperature-controlled coldish water with the ZGAT machine monitoring his temperature as he cooled down. This involved the attendees at the conference (which included eminent scientists) being able to ask questions. This is an element of peer review. One cannot publish a paper in a reputable scientific journal without it being thoroughly examined by scientists from the same field of work. If one gets turned down by one such journal, one might be given recommendations of how to improve the presentation and then to resubmit. The work on sublingual temperature was turned down by the *Journal of Applied Physiology*. Bill decided not to resubmit as it would take a lot of time, and it was accepted by the *British Medical Journal* after we had made some improvements. Bill's approach with PhD researchers was to get to work published and peer reviewed before submitting the PhD thesis. With this approach it would be virtually impossible to fail the PhD assessment. A very reassuring approach.

The 1973 paper resulted in 17 citations. The more detailed 1975 paper has had 69 citations to date (31/5/22), with 6 after 2018.

The third piece of research studied the role of body size, sex, and subcutaneous fat on the cooling of young people aged 8 to 20 years swimming in cold water. This involved 28 children swimming in cold water in an indoor pool. There were about 10 observers undertaking measurements: height, weight, body temperatures before and after the swim, pool temperature, air temperature, metabolic rates (in two), skinfold thicknesses. Children who felt uncomfortable could come out. Three boys had to come out and they were feeling very cold and could not continue swimming. A girl aged 8 came out because she felt tired and very cold. Her temperature had dropped by 1.9°C. One boy came out of the pool early and was still shivering 30 minutes from the time of leaving and had a temperature of 35.1°C. The young people belonged to swimming clubs in and around Wandsworth. The boy mentioned last was used to swimming five evenings a week and with much further distances than the distance covered in this experiment.

There were many numerical readings to analyse. I wrote a computer program using the language Fortran IV. This was a statistical method to test the strength of the influence of one value on another. Bill and I took advice from a professor of statistics on this.

The experiments showed swimming at a relatively slow rate in water well above the usual summer sea temperature around Britain can be dangerous especially in young thin children.

Such an experiment had not been undertaken before. We published the results in the *Journal of Applied Physiology* in 1973. The paper has been cited 180 times, 23 since 2018. The citation which pleases me most is an article published by three scientists including Mike Tipton. Mike Tipton evolved as the leading expert in survival in cold water and other aspects of hypothermia after Bill Keatinge died. Like Bill, he is often on the radio and television. I have communicated with him on occasions. One of his co-workers was Frank Golden. Frank was a friend of Bill's and was one of the observers in this experiment of ours with the young people. I think Bill met Frank when the latter was working for the Institute of Naval Medicine. Frank was also on the television occasionally. Frank eventually became a Surgeon Rear Admiral. He died in 2014.

The article, published in the *International Journal of Aquatic Research and Education* in 2015, is "The Physiological Response on Immersion in Cold Water and the Cooling Rates on Swimming in a Group of children Aged 10 – 11 years" by Flora Bird, Jim House and Michael J. Tipton.

A quote from this paper, which demonstrates how our work is regarded, follows:

> "A seminal paper published by Sloan and Keatinge (1973) observed the response to hypothermia in children swimming in cold water. They found that subcutaneous fat and SA:M [surface area to mass ratio] were most strongly correlated to body temperature. Since then, experiments have been conducted with children cycling in a cold environment of 5 °C/41 °F (Smolander, Bar-Or, Korhonen, & Ilmarinen, 1992), but little additional quantitative data on children's cooling rates while swimming in cold water has been collected."

The research I undertook at that time was in an area of human physiology that has given me a lifelong interest. I think there are very few doctors and scientists in the world who take note of the errors inherent in deep body temperature measurement. This could be due to the vast number of scientific publications, which is increasing year by year. Significant research could be buried amongst this ocean of words. Nobel prize level of research has been bypassed. Here are two examples of significant discoveries being ignored:

1. Gregor Mendel. He discovered the basics of inheritance. He is called "the father of genetics". His work was not read or quoted by anyone in his lifetime.
2. Ignaz Semmelweis. He discovered that surgeons who did not wash their hands had a higher death rate in their patients. He was called "the saviour of mothers". He discovered that puerperal fever (infection of the blood from the uterus) could be drastically reduced by disinfecting the hands. His work was ignored for a long time by surgeons because they thought he was accusing them of being dirty!

I hope you don't think I have delusions of grandeur! I certainly don't think I have made a world-beating discovery that has been buried like in the above two examples. They are at the one end of the spectrum of buried scientific works. The more citations one has over the years, the more likely to the science is to be recognised. Also, it is important that there is a chance for people to disprove the conclusions in scientific papers and find flaws in the method used. It is very difficult to control experiments by eliminating influences one thinks might affect the results, thus decreasing their reliability. One of my favourite expressions of Bill Keatinge is: "It is generally accepted, other things being equal, that…"

This physiology research in the early days of my career gave me a lifelong enquiring and questioning mind. The development of the internet and some training in search methods has greatly helped this. Starting from first principles in the science made me often start from first principles when I worked as a general practitioner and was having to make diagnoses. As I mentioned, human physiology is the study of how the body works. I found it useful to know something about how it worked when it came to thinking about a patient where something was going wrong with his or her body. I have a lifelong interest in hypothermia and body temperature regulation. I was particularly possessed with worries about screening for diseases using clinical thermometers, which were not at all accurate in certain common situations. Let me give a couple of examples of my concerns about screening for SARS and later Covid.

Below is a copy of a letter, written by me, which was published as a rapid response on the website of the British Medical Journal. *BMJ* 2020;368:m406.

"Dear Sir,

Forehead temperature and screening for coronavirus

This informative editorial makes no reference to the widespread use of screening for possible fever using non-contactable forehead thermometers. Almost daily on the TV news one can see the skin temperature of the forehead being quickly measured outdoors. The President of China was recently filmed having a temperature measurement made at his wrist as were people getting on to a bus in China.

Sublingual temperature is lowered by being in a cold environment and slowly rises to a stable reading in a warm environment. (1)

During the SARS epidemic, the temperature screening site was the aural canal. It has been shown that aural temperature is lowered by being in a cold environment, an effect that can be eliminated by keeping the outer ear at the same temperature as the aural canal using a servo-controlled heat pad (2). I warned at that time that care should be taken when screening for SARS so that cases are not missed (3).

Using an infrared thermometer, Erenberk et al. (4) demonstrated cooling of the forehead took place when children were exposed to cold outdoor temperatures before entering a paediatric emergency department. It took up to 10 minutes for that temperature to increase to a steady reading. They recommended that children should be acclimatised in a warm environment for at least 10 minutes before taking body temperature readings.

I recently bought a Fairywill infrared thermometer model JPD-FR401 (made in China). It can measure either forehead (contact) or eardrum temperature. The accompanying instruction manual is comprehensive. "Make sure both user and thermometer have stayed in a steady state room condition for at least 30 minutes. Recent exposure to hot or cold temperatures will impact your reading." I measured my forehead temperature in a warm (21.2C) room before and after being outside (5.3C) for 5 minutes. Repeated measurements showed it took 9 minutes for the forehead temperature to return to a steady state of 37.3C from 36.4C. outside. The operating temperature of that thermometer was between 8 and 40 deg C.

The environmental temperature in Beijing (population over 20 million) is forecast to be between –1C and 10C from 24th February to 7th March.

Measuring temperature from the forehead in a coronavirus screening procedure undertaken in cold environments is likely to result in many cases being missed thus causing spread of the infection."

1. Depression of sublingual temperature by cold saliva. R E G Sloan, W R Keatinge. British Medical Journal, 1975, 1, 715 – 720.
2. Keatinge WR, Sloan REG. Deep body temperature from aural canal with servo- controlled heating to outer ear. *J Appl Physiol* 1975; **38**: 919–21.
3. SARS: screening, disease associations and response. Lancet. 31 May 2003. DOI: https://doi.org/10.1016/S0140-6736(03)13507-6
4. Skin temperature measurement using an infrared thermometer on patients who have been exposed to the cold. Erenberk, U et al. Pediatrics International August 2013. http://doi.org/10.1111/ped.12188

(Links accessed 22/7/22)

I wrote to Mike Tipton (mentioned above) about this.

On Sunday, 26 January 2020, Mike Tipton <michael.tipton@port.ac.uk> wrote:

Richard,

Good to hear from you.

Your concerns are feel-founded. For this to work the authorities would have to be stopping thousands of "false-positives" e.g., those who ran when they left to plane, those who drank on the plane, people with sunburn i.e. anyone who for whatever reason was vasodilated when approaching the thermographic camera.

I have attached a relevant paper*.

All the best,

Mike

*Considerations for the measurement of core, skin and mean body temperatures Nigel A.S. Taylor, Michael J. Tipton, Glen P. Kenny.

Journal of Thermal Biology. October 2014,

This is a comprehensive review article of nearly 100 pages. It is one of the best critiques of human body temperature measurement I have seen, and I have spent decades investigating Google Scholar on all this. Our work on thermometers was quoted here as positive evidence.

I sent my *British Medical Journal* letter and Mike Tipton's response to my MP, Rt Hon. Yvette Cooper and she forwarded it to the appropriate person in the government.

However, in July 2020 the government issued a press release which contained the advice of the Medical and Healthcare Products Regulation Agency.

'Warning: that thermal cameras and other such "temperature screening" products, some of which make direct claims to screen for COVID-19, are not a reliable way to detect if people have the virus.'

Below is a link to the full press release (accessed 22 7 22).

https://www.gov.uk/government/news/dont-rely-on-temperature-screening-products-for-detection-of-coronavirus-covid-19-says-mhra

I wonder whether anyone from SAGE saw my letter. I think there were plenty of other scientists worrying about the accuracy of screening for Covid. In any case, I doubt if these eminent scientists will take any notice of an elderly retired GP sitting at home taking photographs of his television screen!

I took a photograph of my television screen sometime in March 2020. I'm not sure what part of our country the first one was but the average temperature in March 2020 in the UK was 8°C and that includes daytime. This was taken in the evening. What one can clearly see is that the temperature recorded by the forehead thermometer (I cannot tell whether this is a contactless one or not) is 35.2°C. Some scientists have stated that hypothermia can be defined as a body temperature of less than 35°C. I am assuming that this driver did not have hypothermia. However, he could have had Covid!

BBC News. March 2020. Mid-evening

On another occasion, I took a photograph of the President of China having a temperature screened using a thermometer at his wrist. Or is it his thumb?

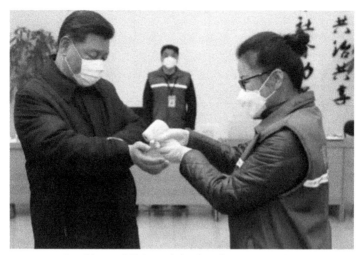

President of China, Xi Jinping: fever screening

I think I have demonstrated to readers that my episode of intense research activity provided me with a way of thinking and questioning medical traditions. It also developed in me a long-term fascination with the cold and human temperature regulation. I have described the care that is taken in planning quantitative research, and introducing a change in part of an experiment must have a control to compare its effects. In most of our experiments, a volunteer was the control for the subsequent change introduction. My work was supervised at a distance by Bill Keatinge, who was also my co-worker.

I have been a member of a strong community group based where I live for about fourteen years. I have chaired a subgroup which deals with health in the broadest sense. There was and still is a diverse membership of people. Some are working on the ground in Airedale, but others work in a management capacity for the Wakefield district. I had never really thought or read in any depth about the difference between quantitative and qualitative research until we had a member of the health subgroup who was keen on action research.

I bought two books at that time:

1. Qualitative research in healthcare. Edited by Catherine Pope and Nicholas Mays. 1999. BMJ Publishing Group. (*)

2. You and your action research project. Jean McNiff, Pamela Lomax and Jack Whitehead. 1996. Routledge and Hyde Publications. (**)

"What is qualitative research? (* pages 3-4). Qualitative research is often defined by reference to quantitative research … an unfortunate corollary of this way of defining qualitative research is the inference that because qualitative research does not seek to quantify or enumerate, it does not "measure"… whilst it is true that qualitative research generally deals with talk or words rather than numbers, this does not mean that it is devoid of measurement, or that it cannot be used to explain social phenomena …. One of its key strengths, is that it studies people in their natural settings rather than in artificial or experimental ones. Another feature of qualitative research (which some authors emphasise) is that it often employs several different methods or adopts a multi-method approach."

"What is action research? (** pages 7-8). Action research is one kind of research. There are many other kinds. Action research is a form of practitioner research that can be used to help you improve your professional practices in many types of different workplaces. Practitioner research simply means that the research is done by individuals themselves into their own practices …. well-conducted action research can lead to your own professional development; to better professional practice; to improvements in the institution in which you work; to your making a contribution to the good order of society."

So, there are many different methods used in qualitative research: surveys, questionnaires, interviews, focus groups, case studies. Up to this time of writing I have thought that qualitative research is a second-class citizen compared to quantitative research. That is despite my having done significant pieces of qualitative research myself! I am wrong. Both methods have the same objective: dealing with the truth.

One of the loves of my professional life was teaching and training prospective and established general practitioners. I was a continuing medical education tutor for the general practitioners working in the Pontefract area. Guided by Dr. Jamie Bahrami, director of postgraduate GP education at the Yorkshire Deanery, I worked with a fellow GP tutor for the Wakefield GPs, Mark Napper, to pilot the training of GPs to become mentors. This training was offered to all Yorkshire GPs and resulted in more than 100 trained mentors in 1998. In time, I became an associate director at the department of postgraduate education at Leeds University. I was encouraged to undertake a research project on the impact of GP mentors in Yorkshire. This resulted in the following paper being published by myself and the new director, George Taylor.

Sloan, R.E.G. & Taylor, G. The impact of General Practitioners trained as mentors a study of mentoring activity and potential. *Mentoring and Tutoring*. 2003; 11; No3; 321-330.

Standard methodology was used to design a questionnaire. The development phase involved consultation with expert educators. The postal questionnaire was used to explore training, past, and current activity, personal needs, and plans as a mentor. Of the 96 mentors trained in 1998, 84% replied., a good response for doctors! The study showed that although mentoring activity in Yorkshire has been low, a small number of mentors have spent significant time helping several colleagues. Most of the GP mentors were willing to continue mentoring and some prepared to work with colleagues other than fellow GPs and travel outside the locality. Some were willing to spend significant time mentoring. A significant amount of work was undertaken by me to analyse the results from the questionnaires and get a paper written jointly with George Taylor, the then director, to be accepted by a peer-reviewed and appropriate journal.

Despite the work undertaken for this study, I found it much easier on the mind than the quantitative work I have described above. This may have given me a jaundiced eye, looking down somewhat on qualitative work. This is because I was taught to question every aspect of the quantitative work and consider any possible bias as well as controlling the study as perfectly as possible.

I am a trustee of a small charity called Spectrum People. The chair of our board of trustees is Dr. Steven Michael OBE, MBA, DBA, RMN,

FRSA. I have read his doctoral thesis as well as a chapter he has written for a book to be published in 2024. He has undertaken a huge and fascinating piece of qualitative research.

The chapter is entitled: "The challenge of sustaining innovation in a complex human system. Creative Minds: a health and wellbeing partnership between the NHS and local creative ventures in South West Yorkshire, England". It is a case study.

Reading this and hearing Steven speak about his research has made me change my mind. I now think qualitative is as important as quantitative research. One reason is that complex systems cannot be controlled like with my research. If research was only done when controlled experiments can be designed, lots of truths would not emerge. I think there might be different personalities required for each of these two means of enquiry.

Are there only these two means of enquiry/research: qualitative and quantitative? I asked ChatGPT (an artificial intelligence site) to answer this question for me. The second answer, 2/2, was more comprehensive than the first. Answers can be regenerated until one can use one. I have copied this answer in full and not altered it, which is simply to show readers an output of an artificial intelligence (AI) tool.

> "2 / 2
>
> Qualitative and quantitative research are two broad categories that encompass various approaches to inquiry, but they are not the only means of research. These two methods represent the ends of a continuum, and many research studies use a combination of both, known as mixed methods research. Additionally, there are other research paradigms and methodologies that fall outside the strict qualitative-quantitative dichotomy. Here are a few examples:
>
> 1. Mixed Methods Research: Combines elements of both qualitative and quantitative research. Researchers collect and analyse both qualitative and quantitative data in a single

study to gain a more comprehensive understanding of the research question.

2. Action Research: Involves a cyclic process of planning, acting, observing, and reflecting, often used in educational or organizational settings. It aims to solve specific problems and improve practices.

3. Case Study Research: In-depth exploration of a specific instance or phenomenon. It often involves a detailed examination of a particular case, such as an individual, group, or organization.

4. Ethnographic Research: Involves the study of people and cultures in their natural environment. Researchers immerse themselves in the culture or community they are studying to gain a deep understanding of social practices and perspectives.

5. Historical Research: Examines events, trends, or issues from the past to understand their significance and impact on the present. It often involves the analysis of historical documents, artifacts, and records.

6. Experimental Research: Involves the manipulation of variables in a controlled environment to establish cause-and-effect relationships. This approach is common in the natural and physical sciences.

7. Survey Research: Involves collecting data from a sample of individuals through standardized questionnaires or interviews. It is often used to gather information about attitudes, behaviours, or opinions.

8. Correlational Research: Examines the relationship between two or more variables without manipulating them. It helps identify associations and patterns but does not establish causation.

These are just a few examples, and researchers often choose the approach that best fits their research questions, goals, and the nature of the phenomenon under investigation. The choice of research methodology depends on the researcher's theoretical framework, epistemological stance, and the specific objectives of the study."

Created by me and AI, 15 11 23.

CHAPTER 6

Bytes and hearts: The evolution of friendship from telephones to the era of telecommunication

For many decades, information technology has been my companion, a key element in establishing connections between people. It has played a vital role with my friendships. Since Kath died in 2015, I feel totally dejected if I cannot connect to the internet at home. This is partly because I lose contact with my friends, by email and Facebook. These methods of communication are an antidote to loneliness. I very rarely feel lonely these days.

I started writing this in December 2020, a few days after I had been interviewed by Dr. Malcolm Fisk. He was researching for his book on telemedicine. He came across me while browsing the internet. He found my blog, where I mentioned my work at Healthwatch Wakefield. He asked Healthwatch Wakefield to contact me with his email address so we could arrange to talk. Malcolm Fisk is a Professor of Ageing and Digital Health at De Montfort University, Leicester. He is an expert advisor to the World Health Organisation on its digital health strategy. You can imagine how nervous I became at the thought of being interviewed by such an eminent academic. He set up a Zoom meeting so we could talk. I told him I was nervous. In advance, he sent me an email attachment with one of the chapters for the new book but also the questions and areas he would like to discuss with me. I felt better with this information. Seeing and hearing one another on our computer screens facilitated a relaxed atmosphere. It was certainly far better than a phone call and I found it just as good as a face-to-face meeting. I got used to Zoom and other similar methods of communication during the Covid-19 pandemic.

Telemedicine. Internet. Blog. Email. Digital health. Zoom meeting. These are all words used in the first paragraph and are representative of digital communication using the internet. I do not want to explain them now but rather at the end of this chapter.

Let me start with a quote of Professor J. Z. Young. I and a few of my fellow preclinical medical students at UCL worked closely with him during a research BSc degree course in Anatomy.

"Whether we like it or not, we can be sure that societies that use to the full the new techniques of communication, by better language and by better machines, will eventually replace those that do not."

JZ, as he was known, and as mentioned in Chapter 2, was an eminent scientist (Vice President of the Royal Society and third Reith Lecturer). He said this in 1950. My interpretation is that he was predicting that there will be survivors of the best communicators rather than Darwin's "survival of the fittest". This could be the basis of a discussion. It does not just apply to the human species.

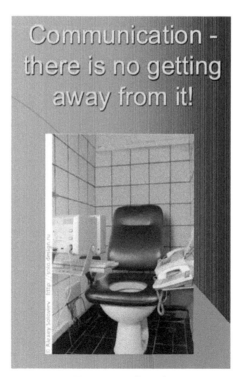

Never out of touch

Information technology seems to be anything to do with the transmission of information. I will describe my experiences with the development of radios, televisions, and telephones first as I feel this is easier for most people to appreciate compared with computers, etc.

The Wireless/Radio

Crystal wirelesses were popular for a few years up until about 1920. My father's brother, Sam, made a crystal radio, and friends and neighbours came to the house to listen to it with him. He lived with his parents and siblings in what is now Northern Ireland. I think he was about 16 and they may have been listening illegally to transmissions building up to the Irish Civil War, which started in 1922. I made a crystal radio from a simple kit when I was a teenager.

When I was at senior school in Wakefield and about 12 years old, I had a portable transistor radio with an earphone. I always sat at the back of the class. I had the phone in a pocket of my trousers, and the lead and the earphone went up my sleeve. I could lean with the elbow on the desk and my hand covering my ear and listen to the radio during a lesson. Of course, I got caught and was moved to the front. A few years ago, Martin, a relation who lives in Leeds, often did this openly during lunches on Saturdays to listen to football match results.

My parents gave me a huge radiogram sometime after I became a medical student and moved in to a flat. It was a great machine but took up a lot of space. We changed flats several times, so it was a bit of a problem when it came to moving.

When Kath and I moved into the house in Airedale, Castleford in 1978, we bought a piano and a state-of-the-art Bang and Olufsen BeoCenter stereo radio and record player. In the 1980s, when CDs came in, I had a Bose VHF radio/CD player in my study. The acoustics of both machines were fantastic.

I bought a new car in 2016 and it was fitted with a digital audio broadcasting (DAB) radio, as is my clock alarm by my bedside. I also have a handheld portable digital radio. Digital radio has a lack of interference resulting in clear audio.

I have had a couple of Bose internet speakers since 2018. They are powered by the mains, and one is in the kitchen and the other is in my study. They were set up using an application on my phone. They are connected to the internet Wi-Fi system in the house. There is a facility to have six preset radio stations. The stations can be chosen from the many thousands available across the world. These speakers can also play audio from other devices using a Bluetooth connection. Bluetooth is a short-range wireless connection between two devices that does not rely on the internet. For example, music can be played on these speakers transmitted from an iPad or mobile phone. I also have a portable Bluetooth speaker, which I can use with my phone in the garden.

I have one of the latest mobile phones, an iPhone 11. It can act as an internet radio connected by Wi-Fi. Speech and music programmes as well as tracks can be downloaded and stored on the phone. These can be listened to when there is no internet connection. The phone can also connect to radio stations via a mobile phone's provider network e.g., O2, Vodafone, etc., again allowing audio to be heard where there is no internet connection.

One of the most sophisticated applications one can have on a modern mobile phone is BBC Sounds. I absolutely love that facility, especially as I am a great fan and user of the BBC. With a Wi-Fi or mobile network connection each of the BBC radio stations can be heard live. If one misses the start of the live radio programme one can restart from the beginning. Shortly after the programme is finished it is available either to listen to later using a connection to Wi-Fi, or mobile network (this is called streaming), or to download to the storage memory of the phone to hear anytime without any connection. Available to listen to at any time or to download are thousands of programmes. For example, the great majority of the annual Reith lectures and nearly every *Desert Island Discs* programme from BBC Radio 4. Many of the programme makers produce extra audio files available to listen to or download. These enhance an interview or give a different slant or commentary on a programme. These are called podcasts.

During the pandemic lockdowns, I have found the radio a great comfort. I start each day woken by a DAB clock alarm with the BBC Radio 4 *Today* programme for an hour. Then I have a cup of coffee in bed reading *The Guardian* downloaded to my Kindle. At the same time, I listen to Radio 3 from a small Bluetooth speaker connected to my mobile phone. During shaving in the bathroom, I listen to the digital portable radio. After showering and dressing, I have my breakfast and listen to Radio 4, preset on the Bose speaker connected to the house Wi-Fi internet. During the morning I go for a walk on a circuit round my garden. Whilst walking, using Bluetooth earphones, I listen to classical music previously downloaded to my mobile phone using the BBC Sounds application or Apple Music.

Television

Many people first bought a television for Queen Elizabeth II's coronation in June 1953. I was 7 years old then and I am pretty sure we had a television before that time. The reason I think that is because I remember my parents watching the Oxford and Cambridge boat race with me. I was making a noise during the race, so my mother took me out of the room and left me in the hall. I could not reach the door handle to the lounge where they were. I must have been much younger than 7 and about 3.

A Murphy V120 12-inch TV cost £80 in 1950. According to the Bank of England's inflation calculator, that was equivalent to £2761 in 2019.

My father loved gadgets and I have inherited that love from him. One of the patients was a Mr. Fred Ryans, who owned a television and radio shop in Castleford. My parents were friendly with the Ryans. Mr. Ryans' wife, Mary, was a patient of mine until I retired in 2005. She died, aged 95, several years after that. She must have had a good doctor over the years! My father always wanted the latest TV and I remember him coming home with one of the first colour TVs bought outright from Ryans' shop. In the fifties, sixties and beyond, there was a fortune to be made from television rentals. The Ryans became wealthy from the TV business and other investments.

My father's daughter Geraldine (from his first marriage) married Johnny Dunn. He was from Glasgow. They settled there and Johnny worked with his father. They worked in his father's garage at first, mending televisions. Their business built up such that they ran a chain of television shops in Glasgow. They advertised occasionally on ITV. This cost thousands of pounds for 30 seconds. The TV rentals provided huge profits. They sold out to the Rank Organisation in the early 1960s for what was regarded as a huge amount of money. Johnny was made a director of Rank. The family moved to a beautiful house in Rutherglen. It had a tennis court, and Johnny treated himself to expensive fast cars. One was a Chevrolet Corvette Stingray. He took me for a spin. My back was nearly broken when he accelerated.

John Logie Baird invented the television in Great Britain. He transmitted from London to Glasgow in 1927 and in 1928 across the Atlantic. He demonstrated colour television in 1929 and that year the BBC started transmissions.

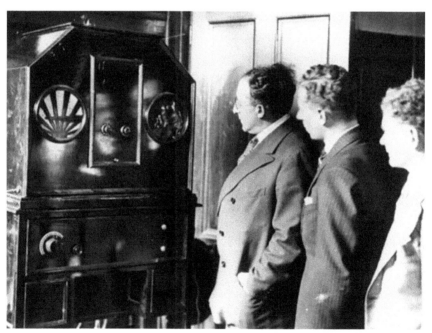

Baird transmitting from the BBC in 1929 (blog)

Independent Television (ITV) was launched in 1955 and Sky satellite TV in 1989.

In 2007 the BBC iPlayer made streaming available, and Netflix started streaming films and TV programmes in 2012. This brief historical summary was taken from a blog from the UK National Science Museum. For a more complete history, go to:

https://blog.scienceandmediamuseum.org.uk/history-of-british-television-timeline/

There was big money to be made from television. This was by both the television programme makers and retail shops selling and renting the receivers. ITV was the first channel in the UK to be mostly supported by advertising revenue. The advertising industry soon realised the huge influence on the general public's purchasing habits that could be made from TV adverts. There has been much research about this influence by that industry. Similarly, politicians and their parties are keen to influence people by party political broadcasts and debates.

It was a breakthrough when TV programmes could be recorded and watched later. A very early video cassette recorder (VCR) was developed by the Amplex Corporation in 1956 and could be bought for $50,000. A VCR was produced in 1976 by JVC and used VHS (Video Home System) tapes. VHS-C tapes were small and could be slotted into video recorders to make home videos. The Betamax recorder, with its own tapes, was produced at roughly the same time. One could buy both VHS tapes and later DVDs (Digital Versatile Discs) with pre-recorded films and TV programmes. This became a huge business with vast profits.

Betamax Tape   VHS and VHS-C tapes

Recordable DVDs   Sky Q multiscreen

We first owned a Betamax, which I brought from Cheltenham, and then a JVC. We gave the Betamax to our friends Grahame and Caroline Smith, who live about 4 miles away. The Betamax was not successful because it was only possible to record for one hour and most films were about two hours. There was a machine which could transfer videos from a VHS to a recordable DVD. I had one of these in my study. Before that I had the 16 mm and 8 mm cine tapes my father and I made transferred to a VHS tape using a specialist local company. Unfortunately, I cannot find the recording. I hope it turns up.

We got a Sky box soon after they came out and I have been with Sky ever since. We upgraded to the Sky+ HD box but I have not progressed to the Sky Q system yet. This is because my viewing habits are simple and I live alone. I am happy to use my iPad in any room to watch live TV. I do not need more screens. The Sky Q box can record six programmes simultaneously and has much more capacity to store programmes and films. I tend to have recorded everything I watch. This is because there is then no pressure to start looking at a programme from the start. I can also fast forward the adverts. I can set up programmes to record on the Sky box using my iPhone or iPad from anywhere when I can connect to Wi-Fi or a mobile network. I usually use my iPad while I am still in bed first thing to set up recordings. I am intrinsically a lazy person.

There is a facility to rewind to where one started watching a live programme but not to the beginning. A live programme on the BBC iPlayer can be rewound to the beginning, as can a live programme on BBC Sounds radio.

I have had a Panasonic smart television since 2017. I do not use or know about all its facilities. I have a separate sound system (a sound bar) connected to the Sky box and therefore do not use the TV sound system. The sound bar can connect by Bluetooth to a mobile phone and other devices. There is a DVD player wired into the system which also plays CDs.

My television showing the Sky menu

The Sky box is on the bottom shelf and the next shelf up has the sound bar and DVD player. Please note the wires behind the TV stand. The untidiness of these drove Kath mad and annoyed me to a lesser extent. With time, the number of connections is getting fewer and fewer. One can now purchase a thin large television that can be wall mounted and connect to everything, including Sky via Wi-Fi. The sound is also inbuilt.

I am not going to write instruction books for all these devices but wish to illustrate the amazing advances that have been made in a relatively short time. The Sky TV guide shown above has 250 Freeview channels to choose from and seven days of programmes are listed, which can be set up to record or as a reminder. There are also premium channels with sport and movies that cost extra. Catch-up TV is highlighted. This facility allows one to download missed programmes and to watch at leisure. The planner shows all the programmes that have been recorded and those scheduled to be recorded.

I download films from Sky, BBC iPlayer and Netflix onto my iPad before I go on holiday. This is a great facility for me, especially since Kath died and I have been on long haul trips. The BBC iPlayer requires a license to view abroad. One can continue to download from Sky and Netflix abroad. It is possible to get round the BBC licensing problem abroad by using a VPN (virtual private network). This can involve downloading an application and requires an annual payment.

YouTube has a wealth of information and entertainment. During the 2020/21 lockdowns I had a Sunday morning routine. Using YouTube, I connected to a live Catholic Mass from St Peter and Paul's Church in Portlaoise, Ireland. I would then watch the Pope giving the Angelus prayer live from his balcony in the Vatican. The Pope's homily is transmitted all over the world. When His Holiness gives the blessing, this is for everyone including those watching on TV. Kath, I and our close friends Kath and Alan have seen Pope Francis from St Peter's Square with the thousands of people who gather each Sunday. He always ends with the words (in Italian) "Don't forget to pray for me. Have a good lunch. Good afternoon," accompanied by a big smile. I think the Pope enjoys a big lunch!

Telephones

My German grandfather, Richard Leopold Friedmann, owned a telephone factory somewhere near Berlin. My mother, Gerda, told me his factory had installed the telephones at the Vatican, possibly in the late 1920s. I wrote to the Vatican to research this but received no reply. My mother's brother, Herbert, took me to the Deutsches Museum in Munich in 1978. Like me, he was interested in telephones because of his father's business. There was an excellent exhibition of the evolution of telephones. This included the first telephone invented by Reis in 1857. It was not a practical commercial phone.

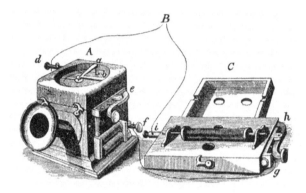

The Reis telephone

I am not going into the history of the telephone but rather will reflect on my experiences with telephones. When I was growing up in the 1950s, being the son of two general practitioners, the phone was an important facility in the house and the semi-detached surgery. The main phone was in the sitting room and there was also one in my parent's bedroom and the downstairs hall. The downstairs phone could be unplugged from a socket and taken into the other downstairs room which Mrs. Price, my nanny, used. She lived in and answered the phone in the afternoons.

A telephone from the 1950s

A bell for the phone was in the downstairs hall and sometime later there were bells on the outside of the house that could be heard in the garden. I think there must have been a bell in the bedroom. The phone rang incessantly from about 8.30 a.m. and messages were written on paper dispensed from a roll in a plastic container. My parents took the messages first thing. They only tore off the long list of visit requests at the end of that session, such that the paper was often over a yard or more long. Then the surgery took over.

Airedale was and still is a deprived area. There were very few private telephones when I was growing up and often the phone boxes were vandalised. There were two or three properties in Airedale where messages could be left for visits or prescription requests. These messages were picked up by my parents later in the morning. The incoming calls to the house and semi-detached surgery could be diverted to another number, such as a partner taking over from his or her home. The facility for diverting calls had been in existence for several years. There were only three GP partners (the third was Dr. Andrew B. C. Smith) for many years, so when Dr. Smith went on holiday my parents often coped without a locum. We sometimes went to the cinema in Castleford when they were on duty on their half day when Dr. Smith was away. A message would be projected onto the cinema screen without interrupting the film: "Message for Dr. Sloan".

Red telephone kiosk

The red telephone box was introduced in 1924 and was made in concrete with the doors etc. painted red. There are two buttons seen in the picture, A and B. One had to have the right change. One put the money in first and then dialled the telephone number. When someone answered, one pressed button A. Button B was to get one's money back if there was no reply or the number was unobtainable. If your call went on longer than the money allowed, you were given time to put some more in. Dialling 0 connected you to the operator, who could make a call for you and that included international calls. The operator would tell you how much money to insert.

You could call the operator and ask to make a reversed charges call. After I started as a medical student in 1963, I made a reversed-charge call from a phone box to my parents every week. When the operator got through, the person who answered was asked "You have a reversed-charge phone call from London. Will you accept the charges?" If yes, then one could have a conversation until the person receiving ended the call, and the charge would be on his or her next phone bill. On one occasion, the operator put me through to the wrong number. A man answered the phone and accepted the charges. I said I that I thought it was a wrong number. He replied, "Don't thee worry, lad. Ta-ra."

In 1964, I and five medical student friends shared a flat in Russell Road, London, W14. We had a telephone, the dial of which had letters as well as numbers.

1960s telephone dial

We were usually careful not to run up a large bill. However, I think it was Grahame Smith, one of the flatmates, who thought up a novel student prank. You thought of a word and then dialled it to see if it was a real phone number and let the person answer and then said "Sorry, wrong number". A word Grahame dialled and got through was 2676352537, cornflakes.

I started work as a general medical practitioner in Cheltenham in 1974. When I was on duty, I had to phone home to see if there were any messages. My first wife, Felicity, was a doctor and did a paediatrics job which involved significant out-of-hours work. Most GP's wives were happy to answer the phone for their husbands and there was a tax-saving incentive to do this. I think Felicity and I objected to all that. There was a facility for diverting calls and I used that. We diverted the calls to Mary Mayo, the general practice nurse. (She was one of the first practice nurses in the country.) I might have checked in from a phone box or waited until I got home.

We moved house a couple of times in Cheltenham. We bought a bungalow at the top of a hilly suburb called Battledown. I was in the sitting room and the house phone rang. The man at the other end of the call told me to look out of the window. There was a car slowly approaching. It was our friend, Bill Bullingham, with one of the first car phones. That was in about 1974. I did not use a mobile phone for work until I was well into my job as a GP in Castleford.

The first mobile phone call was made in 1973. The mobile phone was invented by Martin Cooper, who worked for Motorola.

Martin Cooper

Motorola manufactured the first commercial mobile phone in 1973. It was called the Motorola Dyna TAC 8000X and cost £2639. It could store thirty phone numbers and there was 30 minutes of talking time. They took hours to charge up.

I don't want to give an account of the history of mobile phones but to say they have become smaller and really are minicomputers with a large storage capacity and fast connection to telecommunications technology providers using masts and satellites. The phones can also be used with Wi-Fi.

A pager

There was another gadget that was popular in the 1980s and 1990s and that was a pager. It was small and often attached to the belt of trousers or skirts. It received typed messages. There was an image of flash Harry stockbrokers using these things to do deals, etc., so naturally, I had to have one. I think I only ever had one message and that was from Kath. "Don't forget the bread."

Of course, mobile phones were godsends for GPs on call. In the 1990s when doctors undertook out-of-hours visits, they were done in a car with a driver. Messages were printed out using a fax machine on the back seat. Our mobile phones were invaluable for contacting the base or the hospital to admit a patient.

Towards the end of 2020 I acquired an iPhone 11. It is a smartphone – a handheld computer, one function of which is to make and receive phone calls. I want to end this section on phones by explaining what

I can do with a smartphone, and that might give an indication as to how such a phone works and how powerful it is.

What is the difference between hardware and software? Hardware is the physical device and the things in and used with the machine. Software is programming code stored on, for example, a hard disc, which is itself hardware.

My old phone was an iPhone 7. After unpacking the new iPhone 11, I placed the two phones next to one another, each connected to the mains so as not to risk running their batteries down. (The iPhone 7's battery had got to the stage of having to be charged up regularly each day or run from the mains. This was the main reason for me to get a new phone.) Instructions were followed on the screen of the new phone and most of the data, required software and applications were transferred from the old phone using the house Wi-Fi. Not very long ago, the preferred method of updating a new phone was to ask a provider retail shop to undertake the update in the store.

The iPhone 11 I went for has 128 GB of storage memory and 4 GB of random-access memory (RAM), which runs the software when needed. The large storage capacity was to enable me to store my music and photographs. Let me compare this with the memory on the 1969 man on the moon mission of Apollo 11. The Apollo Guidance Computer was slow, with 2 KB of RAM and 32 KB of storage memory. The speed of a computer is partly determined by RAM. One gigabyte (GB) is equal to one million kilobytes (KB). I will explain further. The smallest unit of memory is the "bit". It can store 0 or 1 (on or off). A "byte" is 8 bits. A thousand bytes is a kilobyte (KB). A million bytes is a megabyte (MB). A terabyte is a trillion bytes, and a yottabyte is a trillion terabytes. My phone with 128 GB of storage memory stores about 10,000 photos, 342 short videos and 2400 tracks of music. It still has 46 GB free memory (2/11/23). A feature film might take about 3 GB, but I do not store these on my phone.

I have the relatively new BBC Sounds application on my phone. BBC radio can be played on the phone and through the Bluetooth speakers in my house. Radio programmes can be downloaded onto the phone to be listened to when there is no internet or phone provider connection. The BBC Sounds website stores a vast number of radio programmes, which can be listened to any time. For example, 98% of the Reith lectures are available. These were first broadcast in the late 1940s.

I have a monthly tariff arrangement with O2, one of the many mobile phone service providers. Part of the monthly payments are repayments for the cost of the phone, which will end after three years. The rest of the monthly payment is for a data downloading allowance using the O2 provided signal. With the old phone, I paid for 1 GB of data download allowance per month. I often ran out of the allowance when I was abroad and paid for extra. I now pay for 90 GB of data download allowance per month, which means that I have no worry about the phone always being connected to the internet. I have no worry about running out of data. I can use the phone to connect my computer and iPad to the internet if the latter is down in my house for any reason.

I have mentioned one application on my phone, BBC Sounds. I have about 100 other applications for use on my phone. An application (app) is a collection of computer programs or a group of programs that perform a task. In the screenshot from my phone you can see some of my apps. One is AOL, which I use for my emails. I can dictate my emails using the voice recognition facility. It is very accurate. Another you can see is the Halifax Bank. I do most of my banking using the internet. There is the Uber taxi firm app. Uber operates in the area where I live as well as in London. My music and photos can be accessed with the two apps at the bottom of the screen. One app informs you of the nearest public lavatory. Kath and I visited our house in Umbria many times. It is situated near Lake Trasimeno. The nearest public lavatory to the house is on the lake's Island of Polvese. The app, which is mainly for the UK, is called "Flush".

Some of my phone apps

I have one of the latest mobile phone chargers. I keep this on my bedside table.

Mobile phone charger

I charge the phone overnight. One simply places the phone on the surface of this gadget. A whole day's use rarely uses more than 45% of the battery. This flat charger gets electricity supply using one of the two USB sockets on my bedside lamp. I use the other socket to occasionally charge the mini-Bluetooth speaker, which I can turn on using the phone. I have a similar lighter charger for travelling.

Think how far phones have developed over the last hundred years. What on earth will happen in the next hundred?

Computers

I was taught to use computers and write computer programs in 1970 when I worked as a lecturer in physiology at the London Hospital Medical College, part of London University. For simple calculations there was a Wang computer one floor down from the department. That machine was shared with people working in the anatomy and biochemistry departments. I worried that I was going to become an absent-minded scientist when I walked down the stairs to use the Wang to calculate 1000 divided by 10! There was an absent-minded professor who died when he opened the outer door for the lift and fell down the shaft.

Wang computer

We had to write our own computer programs. I used a book to teach me how to write programs in the Fortran IV language. I also had help from Fred Smales, who worked in the next laboratory to mine. He had written a program for a game and often "worked late" on the game. (He became Dean of the Faculty of Dentistry at the University of Hong Kong.)

One wrote out the computer program in a notebook and then went to the basement of the building, where there was a punch card machine. Each program instruction was transposed onto cards such that the instruction was then in the form of punched holes or spaces not punched.

Punch card machine

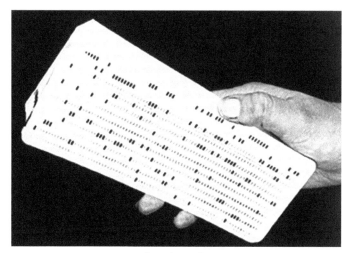

Punch cards

These cards were then kept in a strict order by means of an elastic band and put into a tray in the department. The tray was emptied by someone who took the bundles of cards to the main frame computer at Queen Mary's College, about a mile away. I think he went there on a bicycle. The next day the computer program came back as a printout.

Printout of part of a Fortran IV program I wrote

It was not uncommon for there to be a message on the printout reading "error on line 43". Each line represented a card so that one had to make a new corrected card and once again the bundle had to be run through the main frame computer. The computer program had the instructions as to how to deal with cards that contain data. The data cards were added to the collection of program cards and transported to the main frame computer as described above. Just think about the speed of all this compared with what one can do today, a time gap of just over fifty years.

I have explained what the computer program did in Chapter 5.

I am not sure what make of main frame computer there was in Queen Mary's. The IBM System/370 Model 45 main frame computer was brought out in 1970. It had 233 MB of hard disk memory storage. My iPhone has 500 times the memory storage and is well over 1000 times faster. That IBM computer would have cost millions of pounds in today's money. It could have stored a smallish collection of photos.

A 1970 IBM main frame computer

Computers were not used in general practices during my four years as a GP in Cheltenham from 1973. The prescriptions were written by hand. Working out the on-duty rota was a complex process, and I was involved in that. There were about twenty pages of card with different permutations of duty and surgery times (we worked in a main and a branch surgery as well as doing sessions in factories, Marks and Spencer, etc.). There were four partners when I started. So, there would be a card to deal with when Tony was away for a week that showed how his out-of-hours duty work, the weekly session at Marks and Spencer and his work at Cheltenham racecourse was covered. It was a different card for when he was away for two weeks. We had to work it out such that we each worked roughly equally in the practice. I found this system ridiculously complex and made an appointment to discuss it with a local firm of computer people. Unfortunately, the computer firm also found it to be ridiculously complex and could not help.

A year or so after Kath and I set up the practice in Castleford in 1978, the business bought a floppy disc Amstrad computer. It cost about £2000 in 1980 (£10,000 today).

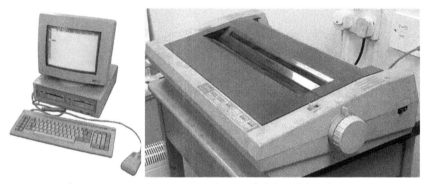

An Amstrad computer   Amstrad dot matrix printer

Data was stored on floppy discs. The image above shows two slots for discs and is a later model than ours, which I think had only one disc slot. At that time the general practice had about 3500 patients and their names and addresses could be stored on one disc. A dot matrix printer had a set of pins that impacted very quickly on an ink ribbon in the shape of a letter of the alphabet, etc. The quality of printing was poor. It has been said to be poorer quality than the first print of Homer's *Iliad* and *Odyssey* in Florence in 1488. I am not sure we did any more than keep a register of patients on the Amstrad computer before the explosion of the use of computers in the NHS.

I strongly believe the introduction of IT and computers into the NHS has resulted in the most significant improvements in health care in my lifetime. Like with phones, I do not intend to write about the history of computers in medical practice. I will first describe some examples that illustrate the improvements.

Each consulting room had a computer and printer and so did the practice secretariat and administrators, manager, and reception. An example, easy to understand, is prescriptions being typed out in the consulting room and in batches in an office for repeat prescriptions, which saves time but also prevents mistakes. In the consulting room a warning would come up on the screen if a drug intended to be prescribed interacted with another drug the patient was taking. A warning also came up if the patient had an allergy to a drug being prescribed.

Vaccination targets for children were introduced in the 1990s, and my partner, John Lee, and I felt that we would never achieve these targets because we worked in such a deprived area. However, we were determined, especially as there was a financial incentive. I was going back to the surgery in the evenings to set up the Meditel computer system so we could keep an eye on the levels of vaccination achieved and work out who to approach. We even went out in the evening vaccinating children, some of whom used to run away!

As the years went on, primary care computer suppliers developed more and more sophisticated software such that everything was done automatically. In 2004 the Quality and Outcomes Framework (QOF) was introduced into primary care. This included many targets which not only covered the medical care of patients but also their mental health and more. It also included the quality of record keeping and other organisational aspects. There was a sophisticated software package for the computers, and reports could be generated either on screen or as a printout. The targets were altered each year. Achieving the QOF targets resulted in a practice receiving a huge amount of extra payment. Some GPs hated the whole thing, but I felt the motives behind the QOF were good. For example, one target was to improve the blood pressure of those on hypertension medication or the blood sugar in diabetics.

I retired in 2005 so only experienced a year in practice with the QOF. There was an annual inspection by a team which included a doctor, practice manager and lay person. I became a QOF inspector and found it interesting seeing how other general practices worked. Without computers this improvement of care associated with the QOF would have been nearly impossible.

General practices aimed to become paperless and patient records were input onto the computer. Inputting the records was undertaken at the start by Joyce Hunt. Joyce was the retired first practice secretary. When she first became the practice secretary, she was unhappy at using an electric typewriter. Kath brought her mother's typewriter for Joyce to use. It was fascinating how quickly Joyce learned to use a computer. All letters etc. from the hospital were scanned into the computer. Summaries were made of the medical problems of new patients.

Just before I retired in 2005, the results of blood tests and other investigations were sent over the internet each day and automatically labelled as abnormal in some cases. In the same year, a system was introduced called "choose and book". The computers in the practice could be used to make an outpatient appointment at the hospital. Anyone authorised to do so could use that facility for a patient in the practice. The service was introduced slowly. We were provided with lists of which hospital departments had come on board. One day I decided to have an attempt at this with a patient. I really struggled to fathom it out and eventually failed. I phoned the hospital department and was informed it had not started using the system yet. Teething problems! I never tried it out again! Shortly after that, patients were given the information to book their own appointments from home. They could choose a hospital and a consultant. For example, one might choose to wait longer at a particular hospital to see a woman consultant.

In the last years since I retired as a GP there have been great advances with NHS computers. Now, my main experience of primary care IT is as a patient. There has been an acceleration in these advances in primary care with the pandemic. Telemedicine is one advance. This includes consultation by telephone or video. Some of my friends do not like this and believe that face-to-face consultations should be the norm like in the last many years.

I will give a personal example. I am diabetic and have a separate problem with my right foot which needs regular podiatry. Diabetics should carefully look after their feet. Podiatrists closed in the first lockdown in March 2020. The podiatrist, Fiona Fearnley, who has looked after my feet for many years once told me that when I was away on holiday and missed appointments with her, I should file my toenails, once a week. When I did this during the lockdown, my toe started bleeding a little from underneath. I could not manage to look at it. I tried using my mobile phone to look at it, but the image was blurred. I felt the only way was to have a face-to-face consultation with a GP. The receptionist said she would arrange for Dr. Anne Godridge to phone me. Anne asked if I would try and photograph the affected area. This was a challenge as I had failed to use the phone to look at it. I then had a brainwave. I found that one could set a timer such that there was a delay before the picture was taken. The delay enabled me to get the area of my foot in focus. I used a facility that was available of emailing a photo to the practice. It looked like a simple blood blister to me, and Anne confirmed this. She asked me to take another photo in four days. I did and it was just about gone. The request for me to do that was OK in the lockdown, but I am worried that, in 2023, telephone consultations have completely taken over from face-to-face. This is a bad thing.

A big problem with telemedicine is that many people do not use the internet. They find it complex or there is poor internet reception where they live. At the same time, there is a significant cost. It is a problem for some of the elderly, who have not been brought up with the internet, mobile phones and computers. Age UK Wakefield is undertaking a fascinating project of lending older persons a tablet and teaching them its use. If they wish and get on OK, they can buy it. We had a friend, Molly (she died not so many years ago), who bought a laptop and learned how to email and send photos to friends. She was over 80 when she started with the internet. However, she got lost when something went wrong and had to be helped by friends. I have another friend over 80 who can use Facebook and its messenger software but simply will not try Zoom. I think she is nervous of making a fool of herself. She had a senior and responsible nursing job in the NHS. I am 77 at the time of writing this. I maintain that when IT stuff does not work, it is good for my brain to try and sort it out myself before using the help systems.

It has taken many years to partially integrate the computer systems in various parts of the NHS. EMIS Health and SystemOne are a duopoly in software design for general practice. Just before I retired, the practice was set up with EMIS Health and I was glad to not have to come to grips with new software again. EMIS is based in Leeds and was set up in the 1990s by two Yorkshire GPs.

These software systems enable data (outpatient records, investigation results, etc.) to be shared with prisons, community care, child health, etc. I had a good experience of this sharing in about 2014. I developed a complex pain and swelling problem of my right foot which was managed by a consultant rheumatologist (Dr. Stephen Jarrett) and an orthopaedic surgeon (Mr. Nimal Tulwa). I had to have MRI scans of the foot and ankle joints taken. The MRI scans were performed in a mobile unit at the private Methley Park Hospital. When I saw Mr. Tulwa, he put up the actual scan on his computer and explained things to me. When I was working, GPs received only the written report of an X-ray or scan. (Actually, we did not have significant training in reading X-rays. This was not so for medical students in Spain, who were somewhat shocked they could not look at the original pictures.) Part of my treatment was to see a specialist physiotherapist. I saw her in a community health clinic in a nearby town. She got my MRI scan up on her computer and was qualified to interpret it. These experiences of mine demonstrate advances in IT that greatly benefit both patients and health care professionals.

One of my fellow trustees at Healthwatch Wakefield (Andrew Kent, now the chair) made a meaningful comment to me a few years ago. He recommended we should stop using the words "volunteer" and "volunteering" about ourselves but rather "unpaid work". We are indeed volunteers who undertake unpaid work. I have had to come to grips with the continuous advances in IT in the organisations with which I am involved. That was especially so in the coronavirus pandemic. It has been vital that I have a decent home computer with internet connection and a mobile phone. I found I could continue contributing to the organisations while on holiday abroad using an iPad and my mobile phone. Until March 2020 (the first lockdown of the pandemic) I attended loads of face-to-face meetings, often travelling to Wakefield, 12 miles away, and occasionally further in Yorkshire. I had a rare one-to-one face-to-face meeting at the start of the pandemic, but the rest of the meetings have been mainly by Zoom or Microsoft Teams. This involves someone (the host) using the Zoom or Teams software, which can be downloaded to a PC, tablet, phone, or other device. A date, time, length of meeting, etc. is decided and then an invitation sent out by email or text (mainly the former) informing of the meeting and providing a link that can be clicked to join the meeting. Joining was a learning curve as the devices we use can all have slightly different steps in the procedure. I had some awkward experiences at first.

At one meeting I could hear and see the other participants but was not able to communicate at all. I texted someone who was attending, and the chair of the meeting advised me to email in any questions to one of the colleagues. Before my very first virtual meeting of Age UK Wakefield District, I asked Diane Wiggans, the administrator, to do a practice with me. She could not hear me very well and I found I had to use a headset with my Mac PC to get the sound right. I don't need to use the headset with the MacBook Pro.

Example of a Zoom screen

The evolution of the computers I have used in my private life started with a Psion Organiser, which I bought in the mid-1980s. It was known as a pocket computer. It did calculations, stored some data and had a diary.

Psion Organiser II

It was also known as a personal digital assistant and was sold as a competitor of the Filofax, a paper-based organiser.

I later replaced this with a Psion 3a which had a QWERTY keyboard and was slimmer and with a modern design. Each of the Psions above were small enough to put in the inside pocket of a jacket.

Psion 3a

The Psion 3a had a loudspeaker that could produce alarms, etc. We had a visit from our friends, the Bullinghams, from Cheltenham. They came with their daughter, my goddaughter, Rachael. We had a lovely weekend. A few hours after they had left, Rachael's voice came out of the Psion saying, "It's 6 o'clock and it's gin and tonic time!" She had recorded that behind my back.

One night, to my horror, our house was broken in to. We were in bed. It was not the first time. My horror was enhanced when I realised my Psion had been stolen and it had our holiday plans on it. I think I had a password set up to start using it. I bought a replacement as by then I had become a gadget addict.

Because the house and surgery were semi-detached, I used the surgery's Amstrad for private purposes. Its main use was to maintain a register of ward members of the then new Social Democratic Party. I stood as a candidate in the local elections and won by three votes after two recounts. I still possess one of the printouts with membership names and addresses.

I did not use any of these gadgets to play computer games but had two units that could be plugged into the TV and used for entertainment. One game was singles tennis. The other was a pistol that shot at a target displayed on the TV screen. We were using that during one Christmas, and we had friends staying. I sometimes get competitive, and I did with the pistol. At one point I went out and knocked on the door of a nearby patient whom I knew had been in the army. I asked him if he had any tips for using a pistol. He did. I went back home, and my shooting had improved no end! The first computer game, Spacewar!, was created in 1961 and used a computer the size of a car.

I can't exactly remember when I started using a PC with Microsoft software but certainly used Office 95, XP, 7, 8, and 10. I stuck with Microsoft until 2015 when I bought an Apple Mac which I have at the time of writing. I started using emails and the internet in earnest in the 1980s. One of the first questions I asked using a search engine was when one of our best friends, Gill Kavanagh, was staying with us. The discussion over our evening meal led to debating the height of Kevin Costner. I went to my computer and found out. He was taller than any of us thought. (He is six feet one inch tall.) I have used AOL (America online) as long as it has provided the email service and at first for quite a while, I paid that company to be my internet provider.

The instructions for setting up and using computers have confused people over the years, including me. When I worked as a physiologist, my fellow PhD student supervised by Bill Keatinge was Jeffrey Graham. We felt the writers of instructions assumed a certain amount of knowledge and that was a mistaken assumption. Jeff and I began to write a book which started from absolute scratch.

An example of the beginning might be: "Plug the three-pin plug of the mains connection lead (see figure a) into an accepting socket. That plug should have a 3-amp fuse. Plug the other end of that lead into the socket situated on the left side of the laptop base labelled M." etc., etc. We did not have time to progress this book idea because we were too busy with teaching and research.

At this point I am remembering my good friend Rosslynne Hefferan. I think she would have been able to write a better instruction than the one I have written here. We were in the same class in infants' school in Airedale. She worked in London for IBM (International Business Machines Corporation) as a technical author. For a few years we used to compare our incomes until I realised she was probably earning more than I. She met her future husband, John, at IBM. They settled in Reading, where she worked in a senior position for Oracle Corporation UK Ltd., which was based there. Her work included writing a British Standard. Well into her career she successfully passed an A-level in Logic. We have had interesting conversations over the years about computers, heating thermostats, software, etc. I have mentioned some of this in Chapter 8.

When I bought the iMac in 2005, I was setting it up one Friday afternoon. Setting up and using computers had moved to being what the business called "intuitive". One can open the box of a spanking new computer device and the only written instructions will be on two or three sides of very small pages with often very small print. Instructions are displayed on screen after turning the device on. The iMac had a "magic mouse". Often the starting instructions are pictorial. It was clever but very different from the mouse I had with my Microsoft computers. I am not sure it was magic. I can just imagine what Tommy Cooper would have said about the mouse. "It works like that. Not like that. Like that." There were no instructions about the mouse anywhere. One had to mess about with it and discover how it worked. That will put some people off. I was not told, but discovered, that on YouTube, you could just about find the instructions for anything. Cars, hoovers, fridges, etc. I think these videos have been made because of the lack of comprehensive instructions for things.

A happy mouse

The afternoon I was setting up the iMac I was expecting my friends Kath and Alan to arrive any time for a few days' stay. The doorbell rang and for the first time I was so wrapped up in setting up the computer that I let them wait and ring again. I answered the door and Kath said, "What's the matter? Your eyes have gone." Of course, I set it up OK and I love Apple devices. I now have trouble working on a Microsoft machine because the differences between the two makes are significant.

As software became more sophisticated, I did play some games, but I have an addictive personality and ended up deleting them. The software to which I was most seriously addicted was Microsoft's Flight Simulator. It was sophisticated and one had to connect a joystick to the computer. The joystick had additional controls for the flaps, lowering the undercarriage, etc. (One of my GP partners, Joti Aggarwol, had an expensive flight simulator control system which included foot pedals.) There were different airplane models one could fly including Concorde. There were written instructions at first. At the beginning of one instruction booklet, it stated "Do not use these instructions on a real airplane." The weather could be set up – fog, a storm, etc. One could have learning flights with a voice saying things like "Too fast! Too fast!" Many airports were available, and one could fly in real time or speed the journey up. Of course, one could crash! My addiction was manifested by my getting up early when I was working, for a quick flight over the Atlantic while the kettle boiled. Our friend Geoff Mair had the same system as I. While Geoff and his wife Zoe were once staying, Geoff and I got down to looking at a flight together. Geoff started a poignant discussion by asking why we were interested in all this computer stuff. We concluded that it was because we were fascinated with how it all worked and that it was a marvel. I have a couple of flight simulator software applications for my Apple devices, but my joystick lies dormant on my desk. Writing this wants me to start having a go!

At the time of writing, it is March 2021 and England is in lockdown. The rules are being relaxed every five weeks or so and currently I am not allowed to socially mix at my house. I can meet one other person for recreation in an open space like a park. The pandemic has restricted us all considerably since March 2020, but there is light at the end of the tunnel with the incredibly fast and efficient roll out of the vaccination programme. I have had my first vaccination (Pfizer) in February and will have my second in April. My IT situation at home has been a major factor in my positive approach and sense of relatively good-state mental well-being. What follows is a comment on that home IT situation.

Mission control

These are the four computers I possess. I have moved three of them from where they are kept to my desk and displayed three in front of the large-screened computer.

At the back is a late 2015 iMac with just under 1000 GB of storage space (Apple). In front of that on the far left (grey and black) is a Kindle with 8 GB storage space (Amazon). In the middle is a 2015 iPad Air 2 with 64 GB storage space (Apple). On the left is a MacBook Pro 2020 with 245 GB storage space (Apple). (I also have an iPhone 11, Apple.)

How have I used these four devices during the several degrees of pandemic lockdown? The MacBook Pro is now (2023) used as my main computer, and I will get rid of the iMac.

Before the MacBook was bought, I used the iMac computer in my study more than either of the other two gadgets. It stored over 10,000 photos and approaching 350 videos. The photos are taken by my iPhone mainly and this automatically synchronises with the iPad, iMac, and MacBook by means of the home Wi-Fi. So, I have access to all my photos and videos on four devices. There is a cost to have Microsoft Word on an Apple device. I have set up a hard disc attached to each of the MacBook and iMac. I use the Apple software application called Time Machine. This makes an initial copy of everything on the computer and then any new items are added every hour. Should I lose data from the PC I have a copy to put back onto it or any other Apple computer. I also pay an annual fee to use Knowhow Cloud. I have used this for several years, and it has files etc. from two previous computers as well as this one. These can be downloaded to the MacBook. The Knowhow Cloud is sold and managed by Currys and PC World.

I am involved with several organisations and during the pandemic lockdowns I joined meetings held on the internet. The two main systems are Zoom and Microsoft Teams. I have mainly used Zoom. There has been a worldwide massive increase in the use of Zoom in the pandemic and shares in the company have rocketed. There was a question of security breaches with Zoom about a year ago. Indeed,

I attended some music recitals at about that time, and one was hacked by someone that resulted in pornography being displayed instead of the music performance. These security problems have been resolved.

Screenshot of Healthwatch Wakefield's Annual General Meeting
9 March 2021 (permission granted by participants for me to use here)

This is a screenshot of a Zoom meeting. One can use the mouse and keyboard buttons to take a photo of a screen on most computers. The little red crossed-out microphone at the bottom left hand of a person's screen means their microphone is off. A black screen means the camera is also turned off. Andrew, our chair, in the middle framed in yellow is speaking.

The Kindle

I have owned three Kindles. They are not nearly as expensive as the other devices. Many more people have got to know the online shopping company Amazon during the pandemic. Amazon owns and manages the devices and facilities of the Kindle. If one opens the Amazon website and look at books, there is an area devoted to books and other printed material that can be downloaded to an individual Kindle device. I download the Kindle edition of *The Guardian* newspaper every morning wherever I am in the world. It costs just over £9 a month. There are thousands of reasonably priced books available to download to a Kindle and plenty that are free of charge. I read a novel in bed at night. I have several non-fiction books on the go at one time.

What follows are the facilities on my Kindle, which is over 4 years old. There are Kindles with more facilities such as fast access to the internet. The screen is unique and uses E Ink technology. This simulates the black and white print of a book but can also show shades of grey and therefore "black and white" pictures. It has a touchscreen used for turning pages. One can bookmark pages and highlight selections of text. One function, which is valuable for a fully certified ignoramus like I, is the linked dictionary. A word can be highlighted, and the dictionary definition comes up. If the Kindle is connected to the internet the Wikipedia (an internet encyclopaedia) definition can also be seen. I have found the device brilliant for taking on holiday. The screen is particularly good in bright sunlight. One can have the audio version of some books downloaded and use earphones. There is a Kindle application that can be downloaded to other devices. I have one on my iPhone and my iPad. Any book or newspaper on the Kindle can be viewed on the app. When opened, it can take you to the page last read on the Kindle. Books do not take up much storage space. In mid-2023, I stopped using the Kindle to read *The Guardian* as that newspaper stopped supplying their daily paper to Amazon. They developed their own application, which is superb. I use this application on the iPad. The cost of the *Guardian* application is also round about £9 a month. It can be embedded in a Kindle application, and this allows one to read any book that has been bought for the Kindle in the past. One cannot download new books directly to the Kindle application for the iPad and must purchase these from Amazon to download onto the Kindle. It takes longer to write about this than do it.

The iPad

Like the Kindle, I have found this device brilliant to take on holiday, especially since I now travel alone. It has enough memory to store all my photographs but also downloaded films from Sky, Netflix, and BBC iPlayer. These can be watched offline. I use Bluetooth earphones to do this. My small Panasonic camera takes higher quality photos than my phone. There is a Panasonic app, available for the iPad. I can transfer photos from that camera wirelessly. One logs on to my iPad by using fingerprint recognition. I was snookered when I cut the end of my right index finger on my razor and had to have a dressing. That iPad had a significant problem in that the battery was getting tired. It had to be used for only short periods or plugged into the mains or a portable power storage device. I treated myself to a Christmas present of a MacBook Pro 2020 in 2021. We have never had a television in the bedroom. However, I take my Kindle and iPad there. I look at my emails and Facebook in the morning before I get up.

MacBook Pro 2020

It will be my replacetment for the iMac in the not-too-distant future. Before it arrived from Apple, I read it up on Apple's website and looked at several YouTube videos which explained its operation in some detail. There was even a video about opening the box which contains the new MacBook! The design of the box is such that it is a stylish experience to open. I was so nervous when it arrived, I did not open it for two days. I had to be in the right state of mind, especially to transfer the details from the old iPad. The instructions to do this were on the new MacBook screen and were quite straightforward. It just took time.

Why is this device state of the art? It has an M1 chip. This replaces the systems that control a computer that need cooling by a fan. So, there is no fan noise with this MacBook. The device is started using fingerprint recognition and the information from two fingerprints can be stored. I hope I never damage two fingers when watching political programmes on the television! It turns on immediately the lid is opened. It is impressively fast. The camera is excellent for video meetings and, unlike the iPhone or iPad, is not set up as a camera to take photos. The facility I am using the most currently is the very accurate word recognition and dictation system. (My iPhone is just as accurate). The stereo speakers and colour definition of the screen make it a pleasure to watch films or the TV. Obviously, the sound is superb using earphones.

Including my phone, the storage space in my home totals 1465 GB. The storage space on the Apollo 11 spacecraft mentioned earlier in this chapter was 0.0000305 GB. The storage space of my gadgets are 45 million times that of the computer that facilitated men walking on the moon.

There are about 100 billion nerve cells in the brain, each of which can make 1000 connections. Not a bad little computer! Perhaps I should add my brain to the total GB storage capacity at my home. However, my brain has a problem. Unlike the other computers, it cannot be wiped clean and start again. Is that a problem?

The memory storage capacity of the human brain is still a subject of ongoing research and estimation, and the exact number is difficult to determine. Some estimates suggest that the memory capacity of the human brain is equivalent to around 2.5 petabytes (or 2.5 million gigabytes) of information.

While computers have come a long way in terms of processing power and storage capacity, they still differ from the human brain in important ways. The human brain is a highly complex and adaptable system that uses a combination of chemical and electrical signals to process information, and it has capabilities, such as consciousness and self-awareness, that computers do not yet possess.

That being said, some researchers and scientists are exploring ways to create artificial intelligence and computer systems that are capable of emulating aspects of human cognition and behaviour, but these are still in the early stages of development, and it may be a while before they can truly match the capabilities of the human brain.

The text boxed above was created on 11 February 2023 by the website ChatGPT, which is a new AI facility. I instructed it to write something about the memory capacity of the human brain. I have not edited it. It was the second version. One can see that students are using this for essay writing. AI simulates the thought process of the human brain to a moderate extent now. I don't think it will ever deal with nuances and will require humans to proofread in case rubbish is churned out. Mind you, I churn out rubbish from my brain quite often.

Finally, I will return to the question my friend Geof posed. Why are we interested in all this? I will rephrase that: What is the importance of all this for me and others?

For the last eight years I have lived alone. The internet has been not only an aid to my hobbies but also a remedy for loneliness and social isolation, as I touched upon earlier. The first time in this pandemic when my modem went down and I was unable to access the internet, I was so anxious that I could not eat. I am not expert at fixing it and that my heating system and TV, etc. rely on the internet contributed to my panic. It was sorted out after a couple of hours. I discovered during a second episode that when the heating system control (Hive) is disconnected from the internet, clear instructions for reconnections are available on my phone. The other thing I discovered (and don't tell anyone) is that my iMac in my study, being just one wall away from the semi-detached medical centre, can be connected to the NHS Wi-Fi, which does not require a password. A mobile phone can be used as a modem. It can be "tethered" to a computing device which then uses the mobile network to access the internet. I pay for 90 GB of data allowance on my new mobile phone mainly to provide emergency internet connection for a significant time. (My last mobile phone had 1 GB). I can also use the mobile phone to connect to the internet where there is no Wi-Fi and access to the mobile network to which I am contracted (O2).

These devices are the "better machines" I quoted from J. Z. Young. Communicating with my friends has been wonderful for me during this pandemic, as has attending meetings using Zoom, etc. I use internet banking and have had a delivery from Sainsbury's supermarket each week. Sainsbury's website is superb. I have done more internet shopping, mainly using Amazon but also the Wine Society, Wensleydale Creamery, Yorkshire Lean Meat, Marks and

Spencer and more. I have used Amazon to send birthday presents here and abroad. I use Jaqueline Lawson to send greetings cards. I pay for my lottery ticket automatically. I book appointments at my barber's. The internet is an extension of my brain. I might never leave my house again.

I have the most fantastic neighbours and we will do anything we can for one another. (There are seven properties situated on the drive where I live.)

Evelyn, a neighbour, and friend

I have been fortunate that, as you have read, I have been immersed in the use of computers most of my adult life. There is a huge gap that has developed between those who can adequately use the internet and those who do not. Evelyn and her husband, Ronnie, are the neighbours whom I know best. Evelyn was a great friend of Kath. Ronnie has helped me no end with practical problems such as light switches, self-assembly stuff, my car and more. I could write a whole chapter about what Ronnie has done for us and then me. Evelyn uses Facebook and its messenger, emails, and has a smart mobile phone. I am not sure she wants to be helped. I think, like many people, she is frightened of using Zoom, etc. I have teased her so much about it that I should shut up. I bought her a book:

Zoom 2020 for Senior Citizens. I told her it was a joke. It took me quite a long time to agree that, why on earth should they have to use the internet for everything, and that they were being discriminated against by the NHS, banks, etc.

Evelyn has a fantastic sense of humour. Why am I writing about her in this book? It is partly because when we discuss the internet, I threaten/tease her that I will include her in a book! The other is that she tells me honestly how she sees internet use now through the eyes of a retired senior nursing sister who has had no need to think about it for the vast majority of her life. I have learned the problems she has come up against with the internet such as renewing her driving license and dealing with the benefits for her daughter, Vicky, who had a severe learning disability. I have tried to understand her fears. The wrong approach with people like Evelyn is to pressurise them. I should not have done that.

One is now bombarded by advice, Covid rules, adverts, etc. that seem to assume everyone is familiar with or wants to use the internet. Telephone numbers are sometimes given out as well as websites and emails. I am sure the way this is done could make a person feel guilty, inadequate or ignorant.

There is special software for the elderly and even a tablet designed for that age group. The Office of National Statistics produced a report in 2019 on internet use. It was the elderly that use the internet the least. Their use is increasing with the years but particularly during this pandemic. Older men are more likely to use the internet than older women.

One rather cruel approach to thinking about the future is to make a predicted assumption that this group of elderly non-internet users will eventually die, and the problem will no longer exist.

If I am to eventually live in a care home and am compos mentis, I want to pick up the directory of care homes and see which ones have the best Wi-Fi speeds and facilities for residents. For the past few years that is what I have done when I choose a hotel.

Computers have evolved to empower us. The internet connects people and is an indispensable companion. Computers and the internet breakdown barriers. They enrich our lives. They offer support. They allow you to ask any question, watch any TV programme whenever you like, listen to your favourite music wherever you are.

These two are good friends indeed.

CHAPTER 7

Politics and friendship intertwined

I have always been interested in politics since I was a late teenager. I had a communist newspaper delivered to the house, and I think I did that to annoy my parents, who were Conservative voters. The only time my father voted Labour was in the election of 1945, which took place less than two months from the end of World War II. During the war years, Winston Churchill (Conservative) was the prime minister with Clement Attlee (Labour) as the deputy in a coalition government. Compared with Churchill, Attlee was a quietly spoken man. A Churchill quote: "An empty taxi pulled up and out stepped Clement Attlee." Attlee and the Labour Party won by a landslide majority of 145, having gained 239 seats.

In 1979 Roy Jenkins was President of the European Commission. He gave the BBC Dimbleby Lecture that year and stated his belief that there should be a realignment of British politics. He finished his term in Europe in 1981. A "gang of four" split from the Labour Party because they felt it was becoming too left-wing and wanted to leave Europe. They were all ex-Cabinet ministers: Roy Jenkins, David Owen, Bill Rodgers, and Shirley Williams. They explained how they saw the future in the Limehouse Declaration. That declaration created a new political party called the Social Democratic Party (SDP). I was a member of the Labour Party at that time. I left that party and joined, along with my wife Kath, the SDP as founder members. Kath was not a member of any party, but, as I mentioned in the chapter on social class, I feel she had socialism in her blood.

Founder Member

This certifies that

....

joined the Social Democratic Party in its inaugural year of 1981

Shirley Williams

Roy Jenkins

SDP

William Rodgers

David Owen

Founder member certificate

Lots of MPs and peers defected from Labour to the SDP including George Brown, the ex-deputy leader of the Labour government, who enjoyed the partaking rather too much of the fermented grape on occasions.

One opinion poll in December 1981 showed the SDP at 50.5%, 27 points in front of Labour. However, that was only one poll. Things moved rapidly in that year. In the summer, the SDP formed an alliance with the Liberal Party (the SDP Alliance).

Campaigning, fundraising, etc were great fun. We spent 1981 and early 1982 recruiting and setting up a campaigning team. Kath and I had friends and neighbours who joined us and did fantastic work in raising funds and leafleting. It was a fantastic gang of people. I was the membership secretary first for my ward (Airedale and Ferry Fryston), then for Castleford and later for the Wakefield district.

We had purchased a computer and printer in 1980. This really was for the GP work. However, I used it for the SDP membership register and still have a printout of some of the members. The first person on that printout is Mrs. Amanda Bateson. I met her last when I was carol singing in Castleford with the Castleford Singers before Christmas 2022. She gave me a hug. The SDP was my first experience of the camaraderie in local politics and community work.

Castleford, and its suburb, Airedale, is part of the Wakefield district, the local government of which is Wakefield Metropolitan District Council, created in 1972. It replaced several borough councils including one that covered Castleford town. The metropolitan council is divided into twenty-one areas called wards, and the ward where I live and worked is Castleford Ferry Fryston or Ward 2. The population in 1982 was about 14,000 and it has been estimated that there were between 5000 and 6000 residential properties (letterboxes!). Kath organised a big fundraising event for the party in our garden. I think there were about eight barbecues on the go.

Fundraising BBQ in our garden

The woman waving is Bronwyn Mills, whose husband, Alan, was a Labour councillor who defected to the SDP. The woman on the far left was Maureen Wood, our housekeeper, who supported us with everything we did. A devoted friend. I think the man in the beige jacket, sitting at the table, is Dr. Edmund Marshall, ex-Labour MP for Goole. He defected to the SDP in 1985.

Raising more funds

We held another garden party which was in the summer and was an evening event. Kath and I were members of the Castleford Choral Society. Two fellow members were invited to sing and are shown in the picture performing on our veranda. Maureen Chapman is singing and the other soloist, Mavis Hunter, is seated. Kath is playing the piano, which we somehow transported from the dining room. Mavis and Maureen are fantastic sopranos and Mavis has performed all over Yorkshire.

The party expanded to cover the whole of the Wakefield district, which has four parliamentary constituencies. We had ward meetings in Airedale but also Wakefield SDP committee meetings. Close working relationship were made at the meetings and with campaigning.

Wakefield SDP committee meeting

This committee meeting took place in Airedale. I cannot remember the man in the white shirt. The others, from left to right, are John Little, Terry Walsh and Colin Strange.

John Little was a painter and decorator. His father was a medical consultant. John lived in Wakefield. He did quite a lot of painting for us both in the house in Airedale and at our second home in Gunnerside, Swaledale.

Terry lives in Agbrigg, a suburb of Wakefield. He is a devout Catholic and became the chair of the Wakefield District SDP.

Colin was full of energy and somewhat toxic about everything. He reminded me Basil Fawlty from the BBC comedy, *Fawlty Towers*.

The party was founded in 1981, and there were local Wakefield Council elections in 1982 and 1983. The Labour Party was very strong indeed over most of the district with only a handful of

Conservative and Liberal members. These established political parties had a well-oiled local election machine. We were amateurs in a brand-new political party.

In 1981 we mainly delivered recruitment leaflets all over the district. In Airedale, Kath and I were joined by friends and patients to become a close team of hard workers. It was great to have some working and retired coalminers in our group. We did not just leaflet in Airedale.

A small gang of us were leafleting in Wakefield when Colin Strange (Basil Fawlty) was bitten by a dog. He had to go to Pinderfields casualty department to be sorted out. We waited for him, and he greeted us with: "It was great. I converted two doctors and the nurse to the SDP!" I certainly learnt a lot about the strengths and weaknesses of a great variety of letterboxes when I was leafleting. Also, questions could be shouted at us if there was a resident in the garden. One question I was asked by a man was "What about hearses?" I asked him to kindly explain. "They are all Mercs. They should be British!"

We started preparing for the May 1982 local elections after the Christmas holidays. The Wakefield and District SDP tried to field a candidate in each of the seats being fought. Two Labour councillors had defected to us in the previous year: Dr. Lutfe Kamal and Alan Mills. Lutfe was a fellow GP working in Hemsworth. Kath and I became friends with Alan and his wife, Bronwynn. I also got to know Lutfe well with time.

I was persuaded to stand as a local candidate and I was joined by Joan Clarke, born and bred in Airedale.

Joan Clarke (Ella)

Each of the twenty-one wards are allowed three councillors. In 1981 all three council seats were up for grabs. I have never got my head round the fact that some councillors are elected for three years and others for one at some local elections. So, it was possible that both I and Joan Clarke could be elected together if we came in the top three. We campaigned furiously for several weeks in April and May. I think we put out about 6000 leaflets four weekends running. We also put out leaflets at the crack of dawn on election day. On the day, Joan and I went round and round the ward in a car with a loudspeaker. I think one of the things I kept repeating was "Don't stay at home, vote for Clarke and Sloan." I did not think that Joan or I had a chance of winning the seat. The seat had been held by Labour councillors since Wakefield Metropolitan Council was formed.

Before the count, we had a Chinese takeaway at home. When I went to collect the takeaway from Wheldon Road I bumped into Bill Clift, an active member of the Labour Party. He had been campaigning strongly. He was friendly with me while we waited for our food, despite our political differences. We became closer over the following years.

We arrived at the count and at the end we had to decide about the spoiled voting papers. This was done between the candidates, and it could be decided that the vote should be completely discarded or given to one of the other candidates. Since I thought there was not a cat in hell's chance of the SDP winning a seat, I was quite generous, giving the Labour Party the benefit of the doubt unspoiled papers. The voting was so close that a recount was granted to a Labour Party request. It was close again and there was a second recount. Of course, that recount was exciting because there was a chance of my winning. I am afraid Joan was defeated. At the time I wished I had also been defeated because Joan and I were such a good team. I won by a majority of four votes and was elected for one year. I defeated an excellent Labour councillor, Norman Kennedy. We were elated.

Wakefield - 1982

Castleford Ferry Fryston (10521)[3]

		vote	share
Byrne G.	Lab	1,899	55.6
Inman W.	Lab	1,678	-
Sloan R.	Lib/SDP	1,519	44.4
Kennedy N.	Lab	1,515	-
Clarke J. Ms.	Lib/SDP	1,060	-
	Turnout	33.0	11.1

From www.electionscentre.co.uk

Kath and I went to London the next day to start a trip to Paris. We were exhausted and somewhat hungover.

I was the only SDP candidate in the Wakefield district who won a seat. Unfortunately, Alan Mills was defeated in Pontefract South after he had previously defected. Lutfe Kamal was not up for election. He was the only other, with me, to represent the SDP on the council.

The next edition of the Pontefract Express had the headline of a short article: "Hair's breadth".

> "Dr. Sloan said the result was absolutely fabulous. He saw much of his success down to people using their vote as a protest, because Labour councillors had been unopposed for so many years. He thought the result was a breakthrough and felt it was particularly significant because the SDP was such a young party."

I think there were over fifty Labour, six Conservative, four Liberal and two SDP councillors.

So, there started a year when I was working hard as a general practitioner and was also a local councillor. There was campaigning in case a general election was called. I wonder whether I took on too much. I had a lot to learn.

Working towards next local and general election: Trying to persuade people to vote SDP in any forthcoming general election, and for me in the next local election was a continuous process. We had one or two high-profile SDP politicians visiting the area. One was David Owen, who was persuaded by Lutfe Kamal to come to Hemsworth, an area of Wakefield where Lutfe represented a ward for the SDP.

Lutfe Kamal, Kath Sloan, David Owen and John Woffindon(?), 1982 or 1983

As the 1983 general election was approaching, Shirley Williams visited. I was a huge admirer of her. She gave a superb speech and the one line I remember was "Do not forget, there is no such thing as a safe seat." She was the first elected SDP MP, winning Crosby at a by-election in November 1981. She lost that seat in the general election of June 1983.

The main media to use for campaigning was our local paper, the *Pontefract and Castleford Express*. It had an office in Castleford, which used to take in press releases. Towards the end of my first year, I met one of the reporters in the office weekly. The press was present at council meetings and some public parts of committee meetings.

One thing upset me and caused me to have nightmares. Bill O'Brien was a senior Labour councillor, and the chairman of the Finance

Committee. I opened my newspaper one week and there was an article about an issue and Bill O'Brien was quoted. The problem was he told the newspaper what I had said on the subject. I had never opened my mouth about it. Politics can be rough. Bill was a good man and won the relatively safe parliamentary seat of Normanton. He received a knighthood after he retired in 2005 to be replaced by Ed Balls.

I did dream about him, and the dreams were not good. I have told Bill about all this, and we had a laugh. I have seen Bill occasionally at Saint Joseph's Church, Pontefract, where he attends Mass. At the time of writing, he has recently had a stroke.

Council surgeries: Most councillors hold a weekly surgery for a couple of hours, usually based in one of the council's buildings. I held mine in one of the schools. One could also be contacted at home. The work that was created from the surgeries was mainly to construct a reasonable letter to back up a constituent's complaint or problem. These letters were sent to the appropriate council officer, but sometimes to our local MP, Geoff Lofthouse, who was a fabulous constituency MP and always helpful, irrespective of which political party one represented.

Campaigns: I was involved in two. One was to prevent a road being tarmacked. It was a road leading out of the private part of the Ferry Fryston estate to a main road (Hillcrest Avenue). I met with the residents in one of the houses and it was a pleasant meeting. I think the reason they asked me to deal with this was because the Labour Party-controlled council was very keen to take this forward. The residents were worried that it would become a through road to leave the estate. The road ended up being surfaced, and I must confess I use it as a through road to get to my house now.

The other campaign was in the council house area of the same estate. There was a road (Keswick Drive) where all the houses had open plan front areas. The residents were really upset about antisocial behaviour. This included knocking on windows, litter and refuse close to the houses and no sense of privacy. The campaign was successful, and fencing was constructed so each house had a private area in front.

That was towards the end of my period as a councillor, and I had learnt a few things. There were over fifty Labour councillors and only two SDP. The trick was to let the Labour group steal your idea and progress it without interference or comment.

Full Council meetings: The most difficult area for me to grasp was that of the finances. Wakefield District Council covers a population of about 350,000, and the money involved was vast. Fortunately, my fellow councillor, Lutfe Kamal, was good at this. As regards the Labour group, I was the enemy. It could be rough standing up to speak at a full council meeting. I did notice that the mayor, Colin Croxall, had a creative approach towards time. I think one was allowed to stand up and speak for five minutes. I noticed if one was Labour the mayor allowed seven minutes to speak. When it came to the SDP, it was four minutes. I went and bought a stopwatch and posted it to the mayor with an explanatory letter. He sent me it back and said something like he was not allowed to receive gifts. Colin was always friendly towards me, which I appreciated. Occasionally, during council meetings, the mayor had to go out to the lavatory for a short while. We all had to stand up as he went out and on one occasion when he came back everyone applauded. There was an area in the council chamber where the left wing of the Labour Party sat, and that included my friend Peter Box (later to become leader of the council), David Hinchliffe (later to become the MP of Wakefield) as well as Frank Ward (one of my neighbours, when we were children).

Peter Box CBE

They will all deny being left-wing, but these things are relative, and sometimes in the eye of the beholder. Sir Jack Smart was the leader of the council, and our Liberal Party colleagues could make Sir Jack very angry by pointing out that he got his knighthood from Mrs. Thatcher.

Subcommittees and visits: I was on a couple of subcommittees. The first was the taxi licensing subcommittee (not necessarily named that). Applications were presented to the members and the backgrounds were read out. We were then asked for any comments. I think the process was private and confidential. I declared an interest when one of my patients was applying. I thought he was a very decent man until the chair read out his court appearances and sentences. I think there was a sentence for grievous bodily harm.

Another subcommittee was to do with refuse collection. We had the task of choosing a new dustbin for households in the Wakefield district. This was before the time of wheely bins. About six councillors met in a smart committee room, which had a large beautiful oak wooden table, around which we sat. Eight different styles of dustbin were brought in by two men and placed on the table. We had to choose one of those. It really amused me because we could not see one another properly and had to poke our heads to the side of a dustbin to communicate.

An outside job: On one occasion, three or four of us were taken by council limousine to inspect some kitchens in another part of Wakefield. Cllr. David Hinchliffe (later to become the MP for Wakefield) was in our car. On the way, we met by chance the mayoral limousine and David opened a window and gave the mayor a two-finger gesture. The passengers of both cars laughed their heads off.

David Hinchliffe

I was elected for one year. My supporters and I worked very hard for my re-election in May 1983. Again, we posted thousands of leaflets over several weekends and did lots of door knocking. I hated knocking on doors, not just because of barking dogs, but also very angry people opening the door! The Labour Party came out in force. There were councillors and their supporters from all over the Wakefield district knocking on doors and transporting voters. The leader of the council, Sir Jack Smart, was seen canvassing houses on Fryston Road, the main road in Airedale. I knew we would have no chance against these very powerful and experienced campaigners from the Labour Party.

We were exhausted when we arrived at the count, but our vote seemed to be holding up quite well. However, we lost. Norman Kennedy was back in. I had several emotions on that evening, and one at the time was I was glad to be kicked out. Norman Kennedy was a better councillor than I could ever be.

Wakefield - 1983

Castleford Ferry Fryston (10698)

		vote	share
Kennedy N.	Lab	2,262	51.6
Sloan R.	Lib/SDP	2,119	48.4
	Turnout	41.0	3.3

From www.electionscentre.co.uk

Cllr. Norman Kennedy

Norman Kennedy died in 2014 aged 70. I asked someone to ask his wife if she would mind my attending his funeral. She was OK with that. The funeral was a very comfortable and friendly event as have been all the local Labour Party funerals I have attended.

The turnout in 1983 was pretty good for a local election, and I felt rather proud of my vote. There were speeches, as usual, after the declaration of the results. Of course, the Labour Party were very pleased with themselves and gloated somewhat. Cllr. Winifred McLochlin said something rather rude and really annoyed my campaigning colleague, John little. He shouted out "Shut up, woman!" She did not speak to me for many years. When I went to the 100th birthday party of the mother of my next-door neighbour, Evelyn Smith, Winnie was there. I went up to her and we had a friendly chat. The hatchet had been buried!

Another speech was by one of our local councillors, Bill Inman. He got us angry by saying he never even got a leaflet from the SDP. We had about 20,000 printed, and most of them were delivered. When we got home, we had rather too much alcohol to drink. I had about 3000 leaflets that had not been used. John Little and I decided that it would be a good idea if we stuffed all those leaflets through Bill Inman's letterbox. So, we set off in my car and I was driving. I was well over the limit. Fortunately, we could not find his house. Two of my patients were back at the house. They were Diane Wormald and

Lynn Rotherforth. I decided that I should be gentlemanly and walk them home to Elizabeth Drive, where Diane lived. I got to bed very late indeed.

The heading in the local paper the next week was: "Norman gets his revenge".

"Cr Kennedy regained the seat last week with a convincing, but slender majority. In losing his seat, Cr. Sloan halved the SDP representation on the council." Half of two is one!!

I continued as an active member of the SDP for some years. I was secretary of both the Pontefract and Castleford branches of the SDP and administered the selection process for who would be our candidate for the Wakefield constituency for the parliamentary election of June 1983. Before that there had been established an SDP/Liberal Alliance which won a few by-elections. 1983 was after the Falklands War. On the back of that, Margaret Thatcher won a significant majority in the general election of that year.

In the 1983 election, Bill O'Brien was the Labour Party candidate for the Normanton constituency. I attended the count as the SDP observer. This was an unpleasant experience for me. There were lots of Labour Party observers. Bill was standing for the first time. Hardly anyone spoke to me or looked at me. At one point, Bill came up to me and said he was worried he was going to lose. Then there were chears when Shirley Williams lost her seat at Crosby. I had to go to the front before the count was announced to make decisions with the other parties about spoiled voting papers. The only time anyone reacted to me was when we were presented with a voting slip that just had "f*** off" written on it and nothing else. I said "You can count that one. It is obviously Labour." The Labour observers laughed. Bill did win, but his majority was only 4184.

I was a delegate for two SDP national conferences. I attended Southport in 1986 and Torquay in 1988. At the Southport conference, I sat next to Dr. Edmund Marshall, mentioned above. We each had a PhD. We had great difficulty working out how to vote for issues as the system of voting felt complex to us – composite motions, amendments, etc. A few chairs along the row where we were sitting there were two retired coal miners. They seemed to have an instinctive approach to a vote. Edmund and I wished we had their approach rather than over reading into the issues. I went to the conference with Alan Mills, mentioned above.

I went to the Torquay conference with Kath, and we made a holiday of that. It was lovely weather, and Kath was brave enough to have a swim in the cold sea. I was a wimp and did not go for a dip! My memories of that conference visit are very pleasant. We saw the Northern Irish BBC reporter, John Cole, sitting on a deckchair making some notes. I enjoyed the fringe meetings. One was by Ken Livingstone, who was a good orator. Although he was "the enemy", I knew how he could have people eating out of his hand.

The highlight of the conference was when Kath and I went to an afternoon show starring Jimmy Cricket and The Krankies.

Jimmy Cricket The Krankies

The SDP slowly lost popularity. There was a vote on whether we should merge with the Liberal Party. I was in favour of that, and the decision was that we should merge. David Owen did not like that and continued with the SDP rump. I was livid and wrote to him, pointing out that we were called a "democratic" party and that he should have respected the majority vote outcome. I did not get a reply.

The two political parties did merge in 1988, and to this day it is called the Liberal Democratic Party. In 1990 David Owen's SDP party was dissolved. There is a re-formed SDP, but I know nothing about it today.

I applied to re-join the Labour Party in about 1990. Not many years ago from the time of writing, Cllr. Tony Wallis told me there was a significant discussion as to whether I could be allowed to re-join. However, I was made to feel very welcome.

I was not particularly active until the general election of 1997 and afterwards. There was a lot of disgruntlement in the party about the selection of our prospective parliamentary candidate. The sitting MP was Geoffrey Lofthouse. He succeeded Joseph Harper after his death and a subsequent by-election in 1978. He became deputy speaker to Betty Boothroyd and was knighted. Later he was made a life peer.

Kath arranged a surprise sixtieth birthday present for me. We were in London to celebrate. Unbeknown to me, she had arranged with Geoff Lofthouse for a tour of Parliament followed by seats at Prime Minister's Questions. I spoiled the surprise. On the day before PMQs, we were on a tube and discussing what we might do the next day. I suddenly had a brainwave! I said, "Why don't I telephone Geoff Lofthouse's secretary and try and get tickets for PMQs?" Kath attempted to put me off doing this, and then came out and told me about the surprise. It was a wonderful experience for us both. We had a guided tour with Geoff's London PA. He had an outrageous sense of humour. He told us lots of gossip, especially about Betty Boothroyd. Geoff met us in the main chamber of the House of Commons right in front of the green bench where the prime minister sat. He told us that members of the public were not allowed to sit on those seats.

Geoff was a great constituency MP and helped me several times with medical situations of my patients. On one occasion he phoned me in the surgery. He started the conversation with "Let me read you this. 'Dear 'arriet, …'". It was a letter he was proposing to send to the Secretary of State for Social Security, Harriet Harman.

Geoff died in 2012 and I went to his funeral. It was absolutely packed. At the very end, there was a poignant silence and a female voice shouted, "Order, order!" It was Betty Boothroyd. I saw her after the funeral chatting to some people. She was dressed very smartly and looked most attractive.

Shortly before the 1997 election Geoff resigned as an MP and I think that some candidates were chosen by the National Executive Committee rather than the local Pontefract and Castleford constituency party. Some members were very angry about this.

I went to the prospective parliamentary candidate (PPC) selection meeting. It was very well organised, and the same questions were put to each of the candidates. One of them made me smile. The question was "Have you ever been a member of another political party?" As you may have read above, I had been a member of the SDP. I thought this was a daft question because political parties spent most of the time trying to persuade people to change allegiances. Each applicant could speak for a fixed length of time. There was a woman from Batley who started with "Comrades!" Hilary Benn, the son of Tony Benn was an applicant. He was a very good speaker. I think my friend Peter Box supported him. I bet he will deny that now! When it came to Yvette Cooper (aged 27 at that time), she spoke, and she had us eating out of her hand, and won the candidacy. She was a breath of fresh air. The local paper reported that afterwards, "there was dancing in the streets". I have pointed out on a couple of occasions to Yvette Cooper that there is often dancing in the streets in Castleford, possibly because of the fermentative grape.

At this time, I was a continuing medical education tutor for GPs in Pontefract and Castleford. I organised a debate/question time for doctors and invited each of the four prospective parliamentary candidates (PPCs) chosen by their party. Each was allowed to bring one guest. The event was held in the Pontefract postgraduate centre. The Conservative, Liberal and Referendum Party PPCs brought their agents. Yvette Cooper brought a retired coalminer from Knottingley. (The Referendum Party was founded by Sir James Goldsmith and was an anti-Europe organisation.) It was well attended despite being held in the evening. One attendee was the chief executive of the Health Authority, Keith Salisbury. Despite his occasional presentations for GPs, Mr. Salisbury was not known to attend GP education meetings. The hot topic for me for this election was the Labour Party's promised abolition of a method of remunerating GPs called fundholding. At a recent meeting of GPs, Keith Salisbury had informed us that it was impossible for the next government to abolish fundholding because it was so set into the NHS. The new Labour government abolished fundholding within months of the 1997 general election.

I am a great admirer of Yvette Cooper, who is an excellent constituency MP as well as a star in parliament. At the time of writing, she is the Shadow Home Secretary. I have helped the constituency and the local Labour Party where I can. I have been included in some of the leaflets. I went to a fundraising event in Pontefract in 2015. There was an auction, and I was bidding for a poster from the 1997 election. I was bidding against the Police and Crime Commissioner for West Yorkshire, Mark Burns-Williamson.

Mark Burns-Williamson

I was determined to get this poster whatever and paid about £100 for it! It has been on my kitchen wall for a long time and is surrounded by cards that I treasure. I have a photograph of Yvette and me taken for her general election leaflet. It was taken by David Jones, a councillor for the Pontefract South ward. He recently retired from the council after a very successful year as mayor of Wakefield.

The signed poster   Yvette Cooper and me

I continue to be very interested in politics and shout at the television a lot. Have I any political ambitions? I certainly have. I would like to have a peck on the cheek from a Labour prime minister. However, I will have to make do with one from the Home Secretary.

CHAPTER 8

A life with bonds

I started writing this chapter on Saturday 17 June 2023. It is a long chapter. My friends have enriched my life. Earlier in the week, there was the expected death of one of my longest-standing and close friends, Rosslynne Hefferan, nee Wheeldon. I wanted to start writing this in the week of her death because it made me think deeply about the friendship we had for many years.

When I resigned from my job at the Yorkshire Postgraduate General Practice Education unit at Leeds University, my colleagues put on a farewell dinner for me, at Weetwood Hall, Leeds. I made a thank-you speech in which I intended mentioning every person with whom I had worked closely. They were all there at the dinner. I inadvertently missed one person out and I know he was upset. I did apologise to him. I will not be able to mention all my friends here, so I hope no one is offended. I hope to illustrate some aspects of friendship and the different levels of friendships as I see them. You will have your own opinion regarding the depths of these friendships.

What is a friend? Since my wife and I were not blessed with children, we formed relationships with many people, and we regarded a large percentage of these as friends. Friends have become even more important to me since Kath died over nine years ago. I am fortunate to have many people I regard as friends.

The online Merriam-Webster dictionary defines a friend as "one attached to another by affection or esteem". There is a bond irrespective of sex or family, etc. Other words used for friend are pal, chum, comrade, and mate.

I searched for "friendship" in Google Scholar. This came up with over 5 million results. Google informs that this number is very approximate. However, one can conclude that there has been a huge amount of academic writing and studies about friendship as well as other references to the relationship. This chapter is not an academic one, as you will realise!

An acquaintance is someone to whom one is not particularly close. It can be a somewhat distant relationship. I believe that an acquaintance can become a friend but not vice versa. There is a similar situation with colleagues at work. Colleagues often become friends. What are the characteristics of a friendly person? Showing interest and goodwill. Cheerful. Comfortable. Empathetic. Loyal. A long-standing friend might be in a bad mood and not be as friendly that day as one's pet dog (man's best friend).

What if one person regards another as a friend and the feeling is not reciprocated? Does that matter? It could be irritating to the person being referred to as a friend by another person whom he or she does not regard as a friend. In fact, that person might not be able to stand the other. A friendship can only exist if each person regards the other as a friend.

Friends can be classified into types. Good, best, old, new, long-standing. I have difficulty classifying my friends and my mood or the passage of time might affect how I regard a friend at a particular moment.

The following first verse of a famous English hymn is food for thought:

> There's A Friend for Little Children
> Above the Bright Blue Sky,
> A Friend That Never Changes,
> Whose Love Will Never Die:
> Unlike Our Friends By Nature,
> Who Change With Changing Years,
> This Friend Is Always Worthy
> The Precious Name He Bears.

The friend is Jesus. His friendship is related to love, as illustrated by this biblical quote:

"Greater love has no one than this, that someone lay down his life for his friends." John 15:13

The relationship between a believer and Jesus can be a combination of friendship and love like is often experienced in marriages or partnerships. Jesus has been my friend since 2016.

A person in love with another often says that the latter is his or her best friend even after the relationship has existed for many decades. Perhaps the friendship aspect strengthens with time in a solid marital or partners' relationship.

George Goodenough

George

I was born eight months before George. The Goodenough family lived 2 miles away in Castleford town. George's mother, Hannah, was Austrian and my mother, German. A great friendship was built between our two families. George's father co-owned a garage in Castleford and he and his partner created a successful business. George's parents had three further children, Alan, Robin, and Helen.

I recently met George at Helen's house to celebrate his seventy-seventh birthday. He has a much better memory of our past together than I. When we were children, the two families got together most Sundays for afternoon tea, alternating between our house and theirs. Sometimes we went a short way into the countryside (Hook Moor) and had a picnic and played. In the winter, we went to the hill in Aberford to sledge after significant snow had fallen. We grew up together and did many things together. George went to Castleford Grammar School and I to QEGS. One Christmas, when we were about 10 years old, I realised, for the first time, how careful George would be with his money and possessions. One of his presents was a giant tube of sweets called Smarties. He opened the tube and emptied out a large number onto a table and said to me "Choose one". He is now one of the most generous people I know.

Of course, we each had other good friends when we were children and teenagers. Late in our teens George joined me and some of my friends on a holiday youth hostelling in Southern Ireland.

George went to Manchester University and I to London. From that point onwards, we did not meet so much. George was made redundant from a job as an industrial chemist and undertook teacher training. He had a job in London as a teacher when I was there, and we occasionally got together. He went back home to Yorkshire every weekend. I think we lost touch somewhat for several years, but our bond of friendship remained. When Kath and I re-established the medical practice of my parents in 1978, we started getting together again as George lived not so far away. He, Robin, and Alan became my patients. I was building the practice up from scratch and was so grateful to them and other friends for joining the list. He was the only patient I told could use my private number for medical matters. He lived about 12 miles from the surgery and never had a visit. He only phoned me once on my mobile about a medical matter in the twenty-seven years I was his GP.

I, George, his siblings, and their spouses get together once or twice a year for lunch. This is either at my house, George and Jean's or Helen and Colin's. Helen is a great hostess, and I am very fond of her. When we/I get together with them, I experience a warm feeling and am completely at ease. I think we all are. They are a fantastic family who support one another to the full. Alan and Marie have a daughter, Jenny. Well into her medical student training she had a teaching attachment to me to experience general practice. I was her supervisor. She resisted all our pressure to consider a career in general practice. She is now a successful consultant plastic surgeon.

I could write a lot more about this family and George. This is an example of a childhood friendship that has endured and matured over seventy-seven years. It does not matter how often we meet. When George and I greet each other I can feel the strong friendship bond in our handshake.

The late Rosslynne Hefferan nee Wheeldon

Rosslynne

Rosslynne was born about seven weeks before me. We were in Mrs. Abbott's class at the infant school in Airedale. That is when we first met! This was not, like with George, a childhood friendship. Boys did not really fraternise with the girls until a much later age. My parents were the GPs of Rosslynne's parents and their family. A friendship had developed between them. The friendship was stronger between

Rosslynne's mother (known as May Kirby) and my father. This friendship started during my father's first marriage. Mrs. Wheeldon was a very good businesswoman, and their house was attached to a grocery shop. Rosslynne had two older sisters, Elizabeth and Judith. She also had a younger brother, William. I was friendly with William and was invited to parties at their house, and William came to some of my birthday parties. I remember well a particularly clever party trick Mr. Wheeldon (Bill) used to do with us. I was blindfolded and then stood on a box. Mr. Wheeldon then said that I was floating, slowly, higher, and higher. He continued to say that until the top of my head contacted "the ceiling". It was very believable for a little boy. What had happened was that he simply patted the top of my head with a book or something similar. The others all laughed their heads off.

The three sisters went to Wakefield Girls' High School and I and William to QEGS. Both schools were direct grant schools. To be admitted, there was an entrance exam, and some moderate fees were paid. The schools are now merged and are proper public schools with high fees. For ten years I travelled to school on the bus from Castleford to Wakefield. It was the 68 double-decker bus and it left from a side street off Carlton Street. Two buses left, one at 7.55 a.m. and the other at 8.00 a.m. The journey took about 35 minutes. Rosslynne went on the 7.55 a.m. bus and I and Paul Simpkin the 8.00 a.m. or vice versa. I cannot remember exactly. Her brother, William, usually sat behind us on the top deck, and was in the habit of firing pellets at us, using a rubber band. I travelled on this bus for about ten years and calculated this was approximately 24,000 miles. There was a "sixth form club" which was held regularly andjointly between the girls and boys after school. The main thing I remember about that was playing doubles table tennis and my partner was Sally Plummer. I had a crush on her. However, I was a very shy person and still am really. I hadn't the guts to ask Rosslynne out at that stage. In any case, she tended to aim high and had a thing about our head boy, Bill Hartley. Both Rosslynne and I went to London University, she to King's College, and I, to University College. Our friendship really started during our time in London. She came to my eighteenth birthday party and my twenty-first, both held at Tieve Tara, our house. I still have a card from Bill Hartley, explaining why he could not come to the first party. Rosslynne's parents put up several of my friends for the night after my twenty-first.

It was London that was the start of our meaningful lifelong friendship. A lifelong friendship has been defined by the depth of the friendship rather than its length. At the start of university life, she lived in a hall of residence for women called Nutford House aka The Nuthouse. In 1964 the girls had to obtain a pass to be out in the evening and had to be back by something like 10.30 p.m. Rosslynne was very attractive with a great sense of humour and a delightful personality. Most of my friends fell for her! One, Geoff Mair, was devastated when they broke up. I used to warn my male friends that she would break their hearts!

I went out with four women students while I was in London. The first was Diana (see below) and the second and third were Kath and Jo. The fourth was Felicity. Rosslynne introduced me both to Kath, and, later, Felicity. I asked Kath to marry me. She turned me down and our relationship ended. She was right. We were too young. However, it was not the end of the story of me and Kath. Jo Trowell was a lovely girl who lived in the flat downstairs from ours at the time. I did not go out with her for long before I started going out with Felicity. We married and lived in Cheltenham. I started as a GP there and Felicity became a GP sometime afterwards. After seven years, the marriage broke down and we divorced. I lived alone for a while, and I could not get Kath out of my mind. I was pretty sure she would be married by then. I telephoned Rosslynne, who was still in touch with Kath. She was not married! Rosslynne gave me Kath's telephone number. I was so nervous to phone her that I had to resort to some brandy for Dutch courage. To my delight, Kath agreed to go out for dinner with me in London, where she worked. Her flatmates knew that would be "it" as soon as she put the phone down on me. It was "it". We married in 1978.

By this time, Rosslynne and her husband, John, lived and worked in Reading and had three boys, Michael, Andrew, and Peter. We started to get together twice a year. They usually came up to Yorkshire every Easter and we visited them later in the year. Rosslynne had a very successful career with the computer company Oracle. Trivial Pursuit was the order of the evening. Thank God John was my partner in this. As Kath used to say to me, "I am astounded at the depth of your ignorance."

Rosslynne came to Kath's funeral just over nine years ago. Kath died after an unexpected short illness. I spent a New Year with them after that and it was good that Rosslynne's sister Judith was there. Judith had lost her husband, Bob, some time before that. I kept in touch with Rosslynne mainly by phone and an occasional email. She kept an eye on my Facebook pages.

Peter phoned me mid-May 2023 to tell me that Rosslynne was terminally ill with bone cancer and was in hospital. I was on holiday on the Isle of Wight with friends, Steve and Grahame. I was just about to get into the car to do some sightseeing with them when I answered the phone. After Peter hung up, I got in the car and burst into tears. My friends understood. Both knew Rosslynne. We three were students together. In the afternoon we visited the Catholic Quarr Abbey. I lit a candle for her, and Grahame shared the cost of the contribution. Her funeral was on 5 July 2023.

May she rest in peace.

Jennifer Doncaster nee Oates

Jennifer and her daughter, Sarah, 2017

The Oates family moved into the house next door when Jennifer and I were 9 years old. Her father was an under manager of one of the collieries. He later became a manager and they had to move to another coal board house after ten years, when Jennifer and I were 19. Their next house was within walking distance of ours. I was mainly friendly with her brother, John, who was a little older than me. I do not remember boys having anything to do much with the girls at the age of 9! Jennifer is only a few days older than me. We became much closer as friends when we were late teenagers and occasionally went out together. On one occasion, I had far too much alcohol, and when we got back to her house, her mother insisted I stayed the night. I slept in Jennifer's bedroom and the wallpaper had ballet dancers as part of the design. I was suffering from "the sittee uppies" and the ballet dancers seem to be dancing up and down. My mother was so angry with me because she maintained no one phoned her up to say where I was. I have never seen my mother so upset. I think Jennifer's mother did phone up, but my mother had misheard the message. I think we were about 18 years old at the time.

We lost touch for many years until Kath and I came up to Castleford for me to work as a GP. It was after that that our friendship blossomed. Jennifer and her husband, Tom, knew what stress Kath and I were experiencing with my building up a new medical practice. We met mainly for meals at one another's houses. We went on holiday to Majorca with them and some other old friends.

Kath and I let Jennifer and her family, including their sons, use our second home in Gunnerside, Swaledale, whenever they wanted. We owned that house for nearly twenty years. We did not charge our friends to use the house. One of their sons, Richard, after he married and had children, regularly holidayed there. I remember him telephoning to book another stay and was really upset when I told him we were selling. Jennifer always took her mother, Peg, who loved the Yorkshire Dales. Richard has been renovating houses and the first one he bought was in the seaside town of Staithes. Richard offered me that house for a gratis stay. He has another small property in Keld, Swaledale. He is creating a property portfolio.

205

I cannot express enough my gratitude for the fantastic friendship that has developed between Jennifer's family and me since Kath died. Jennifer and Tom included me with a group of friends, most of whom I already knew. We went out for lunch, nearly every Friday evening, usually to a pub. The nine of us went on the P&O *Azura* cruise ship for a holiday that took in the Norwegian Fjords. We have been on several cruises since 2015, and lately I have been joining Tom, Jennifer, and Sarah in rented accommodation in places like the Lake District and North Yorkshire. We are repeating a holiday for a week in Barnard Castle in 2024. We all went to London to see the show *Matilda* not so long ago.

In September 2006, Kath became a Catholic. In the year of Kath's death, in 2015, I decided to become a Catholic. My induction was undertaken jointly by Father Simon, the priest, who had undertaken Kath's funeral, and Alan Franks, a relation of Jennifer's who I knew when I was younger, but I got to know better as he and his wife, Honor, were patients. I became a close friend of Alan, especially after Honor died from a brain tumour. We had an hour or two every Tuesday evening at his house to discuss Catholicism and other matters. He was a retired teacher. I think we helped one another with our bereavements. I never thought I would feel bereaved again so soon, but Alan died in 2016. I was honoured to be asked by Kate, his daughter, if I would read at the funeral. Kate and her husband, Darren, are good friends.

Alan Franks, a cruise, 2016

Jennifer and Tom have a group of friends they have known for many decades. Kath and I knew most of them. In the early 1980s, Kath and I went on holiday to Majorca with Jennifer and Tom as well as Judith and Tony, two of that gang. When our dog, Sindy, made a mistake with her family planning arrangements, she had five puppies. Bruce, a neighbour's dog, got into our garden while I was neglecting my role in her contraception by relaxing in the kitchen with a cup of coffee. We gave all but one puppy away. Our friends Sandra and Jack had one, and Tony and Judith had another. We kept the strongest male, Ben. When the puppies were a year old, we had a dogs' birthday party. At the party, the dogs were not the slightest bit interested in the mother and tried to make friends with the siblings by sniffing the appropriate parts of one another's anatomy. Kath and I certainly had a relationship with each of the three dogs we owned, which I am sure was a friendship. The features of friendship with dogs include affection, loyalty, companionship, and protection.

When we were young teenagers, I was playing with Jennifer and John in their garden. The priest arrived, and they vanished indoors and left me with no one to talk to and rather upset. Jennifer used to call me" a heathen".

One must be sponsored by someone to become a Catholic and that person is involved in the Mass that takes one into the church. I asked Jennifer to be my sponsor. She had to stand behind me and place one hand on my shoulder while I made some promises. I was so nervous that one of my legs started shaking, and I wondered whether she could feel that. I started attending Mass on Sunday mornings and sat with Jennifer, Tom, and Sarah. When Covid resulted in a lockdown, we communicated by email, and this evolved into a daily email. This exchange continues to this day. Just about every evening, after I have finished my supper, I email Jennifer about my day and other thoughts, and she replies later. Tom and Jennifer are amazing parents to their daughter, Sarah. They will be rewarded in heaven.

Kathleen Sanders and Felicity Sutton

Kath is my late wife (2015) and Felicity my ex-wife. I will not write about them here. Of course, each was my friend, and I loved them both. The ending of these marriages resulted in differing states of bereavement for me.

Friends from student days

Several years ago, I was asked by the Airedale Academy to teach two lessons to a class of students aged about 15. The aim of the lessons was to tell them about how to become a doctor, and the objective was to encourage some of them to think about doing that. I ended my bit by saying that, on reflection, the best thing about university and medical school is the friends one makes. It is not just about going out to the pub together, but also, and more importantly, the conversations, mutual support, and camaraderie. Most of us have developed interests and hobbies outside the subject we studied or the work we undertook.

My medical student learning started in 1963 at University College London and was for three years. This was followed by three years' clinical work at the London Hospital, Whitechapel. Over those six years I made a lot of friends and some of them are still friends now. Sadly, some have died.

University College London

In the first few months at University College London, we formed a gang of students who did things together.

The gang. From left to right: Sheila Hall, Gill English, Jim Smeeton, Grahame Smith, and Diana Norkett. Below: Geoff Mair

The photo is of some of the gang on a walk at Symonds Yat in the Wye Valley, Herefordshire. Steve Haggie, Jenny Voke, Colin Parker, Abdul Paliwala and I are missing from the photo. Steve took the photo. Steve recently told me that while they were resting at the place where the photo was taken, a group of girls, Brownies, appeared and were singing a jolly song. Sheila pointed out that they were flat. Geoff said, "They usually are at that age."

| Colin | Steve | Jenny | Abdul |

Diana Cooke nee Norkett

Diana (Di) was an undergraduate with us at UCL for eighteen months and then went on to undertake her clinical training at St George's Hospital. We started going out together. She was, and still is, a kind and cultured person. She introduced me to her parents at their home, which I think was near Box Hill in Surrey. I was intrigued that her father was an expert in mosses. In 1958 he discovered a new moss in Wales, Fissidens celticus. He was a scientist and worked at the Science Museum in London. I ended our relationship when I met Kath and have always felt bad about that. Many years ago, some of this gang had a reunion in a hotel in Huntingdon. Kath and I went, as did Diana. It was nice to see her again. I think that was the last time I saw her until 2022.

When Kath died, Di sent me a lovely letter and another communication at the time of the funeral. We exchanged Christmas cards. It was in the pandemic in 2020 that we started writing emails to one another regularly. It is the slowest regular communication I have ever heard of. I send her an email and a month later she replies and so on. I missed one month (June 2023), which is unforgivable.

One of my school and medical school friends, Colin, lived with his wife, Ann, near Tavistock in Devon. He developed multiple sclerosis when he was 58, and sadly, died early in 2023 at the age of 77. I have been attending a reunion of a group of people who met through being students at the London Hospital Medical College. Two of those reunions were held recently near where Colin lived, so he could be with us. Di lives in Plymouth, which is not that far away from Tavistock. In October 2022 Di and I met for lunch in a lovely restaurant in the dock area of Plymouth. For some reason, I was nervous about this meeting, but came away with a warm feeling. This friendship never died with time but is different now.

Jim Smeeton

After spending the first term in London in digs with Colin Teasdale (see below), Jim and I rented a one-bedroom flat in York Street, just off Baker Street. This was close to UCL – two stops on the tube after a 2-minute walk to Baker Street tube station. Jim was a religious person at that time. I was not. I remember the first night we were lying in our beds. Jim started reading a book. I asked him what he was reading. It was the Bible. I thought to myself "not another religious maniac!" It was I who was the odd one out. The other remarkable thing about Jim is that he could knit.

We were great friends, and on the same dissection table. He was one of the gang who knocked about together. However, he went further afield to find a girlfriend. One was called Claire, and she was studying maths at Reading University. She was a brilliant mathematician. The final exam paper for her gave the instruction "answer as many questions as you can". She answered enough questions to get enough marks to be awarded a first-class honours degree. There were enough marks left over for an upper second as well! One holiday, four of the men from our group hired a boat on the Thames for a week and eventually stopped in Reading and met Claire and some of her friends. Another of Jim's girlfriends was Sarah, a stunning redhead. She may have been a friend of Rosslynne's. Some of our gang queued up all night to pay our respects to Winston Churchill's lying in state in Westminster Hall. It was at the end of January 1965. The thing I remember most about the queueing was that Sarah dropped one of her contact lenses. It was a major exercise, trying to find it in a moving queue. Jim married Liz and became a general practitioner.

We exchanged Christmas cards and that was the extent of our relationship for decades. Kath and I were invited to lunch by Steve and Gill, who settled down not far from us in Rotherham. (Yes, Steve married Gill who is in the photo.) We were just about to eat when the doorbell rang, and a couple came in. I did not recognise either of them. Then I realised it was Jim and Liz and my brain somehow sorted itself out. It was as though Jim's face changed into a recognisable-by-me form. It was lovely to see them.

Jim died in his prime from prostate cancer. When we were students, I was a bit hard for cash at one time. I sold half of a premium bond to Jim for 50p. He kept the bond. After his death, Liz wrote to me and enclosed the premium bond. I told her that we should own half each, and that if it won, we would share the winnings. It has not won yet.

Grahame and Caroline Smith, Steve and Gill Haggie, Colin and Liz Parker

Grahame, Jim, and I were allocated to the same dissection table (part of learning human anatomy was to dissect a donated human, six students to a table). The 120 or so students were alphabetically allocated to these tables. Our surnames began with the letter S. Grahame and I also worked as a pair in the pharmacology practical classes.

Grahame, Steve, Jim, and I shared a flat in Powis Terrace, Notting Hill. We shared a large bedroom for four. On one occasion, we had mice and we each bought a mouse trap. On another occasion, there was a rat in the kitchen, and we had to get the rat man in. Thinking of rats, at that time, there was a notorious and wealthy landlord in London called Peter Rachman. He rented out sordid flats (some in our street) and ran brothels. He was not our landlord, but one Sunday we read in the newspaper about "goings on" in Powis Terrace. We were completely oblivious of all that. I recently discovered that David Hockney lived in Powis Terrace at the same time as us.

We will never forget the time I lent my Hillman Imp car to Jim to take his girlfriend back to Paddington Station. The next morning my car was gone – stolen. A few days later, Steve (the cleverest of we four) noticed a Hillman Imp, the same colour as mine, parked in our street. It had not moved for days. My car key fitted that car. Jim had got into the wrong car at Paddington Station and drove it back to the flat. It was an amazing thing that the key fitted two different cars. It was a bit awkward explaining to the police.

Grahame married Caroline. She was a nurse at the London Hospital, but I never came across her there. I lost touch with them while I was working in London and Cheltenham. Grahame became a general practitioner four miles from me in Pontefract. Kath and I bought the house and surgery from my mother in 1978. We then set up a general practice from a zero-patient base. My father had died in 1967 and my mother had retired. Two of the very first patients to join the practice were Grahame and Caroline. What a fantastic act of friendship! Caroline was pregnant and told me she would like a home delivery. I was responsible for her care during labour and delivery. All went well, thank goodness, as the midwife, Sister Pearson, calmly delivered their third child, Amy.

When I was under considerable pressure with my out-of-hours commitments, Grahame and his partners offered to include me in their rota. Another act of professional friendship between colleagues. One Saturday, I was feeling very ill from stress and could not find any help to cover my work. I telephoned a consultant, Jean Wharton, to see if she knew anyone who could help me. I burst into tears on the phone. She called Graham's practice, and the duty doctor was the senior partner, John Waring. He called my house and advised me to stop work for a while. He tried to find someone to cover me that day and the rest of the weekend but failed. He took over my work for the weekend himself. What a fantastic thing to do as a colleague.

Kath and I became patients at Grahame's practice. We dealt with one another's medical problems in our homes. We tried very hard, and I think we succeeded, in behaving professionally with one another during a consultation. We got together over the years for meals, which sometimes included Steve and Gill or Geoff and Zoe.

Later, in London, Grahame, Steve, Jim, Colin, and I had a flat in Russell Road, Kensington, which was near Olympia. Steve went out with Gill, a fellow medical student, and eventually they got married. We went on holiday together to the Scilly Isles two years running. We hired a large house. Our friendships became firm ones from living together, going on holiday, visiting one another's parents, etc. These friendships have lasted sixty years. Four of us have been going away for a few days for each of the last few years. We have been to Germany, Orkney, the Isle of Man, Seahouses, and the Isle of Wight.

L to R – Grahame, Steve, Colin, me
The Isle of Man

The London Hospital, Whitechapel

Kevin Pavey and Colin Teasdale

Me, Kevin, and Colin (seated)

Kevin and I were in the same class in the junior school at Queen Elizabeth Grammar School, Wakefield. We were about 6. Kevin left later and was at another school for some years before he rejoined the senior school. Colin was at school in Normanton and joined the Wakefield school in the first year of the sixth form. They were both much cleverer than I. Indeed, Kevin was an all-rounder for O levels and could not decide which class to join in the sixth form. He started studying classics for a short time until he joined Colin and me in the biology class with Dr. Brian Fletcher, our class and zoology teacher. Colin's younger brother, Eric, was also educated at the school and became a doctor. (See Chapter 2.) Kevin's father was the religious instruction teacher at the school. If we misbehaved, he had a habit of hitting us on the top of our heads with the bowl of his pipe – the closed end of the pot chamber, of course!

The three of us decided to apply to London medical schools without telling the headmaster. He was not very pleased but did support us. We each applied to the London Hospital Medical College, Whitechapel. I got turned down and the other two were accepted.

Here is the reason why I was turned down: Colin was interviewed immediately before me. He was asked the question "Who do you think is the better student you, or Richard Sloan?" He answered that it was himself. I was asked that same question about Colin. I answered it was him. What a swine Colin was!! We both told the truth. After I finished my three years at University College London, the professor of anatomy, J. Z. Young, obtained another interview for me at The London and I was accepted without fuss. The chair of the interviewing committee was Sir John Ellis, the dean and the same person who headed the panel when I was turned down. Colin and I spent an extra eighteen months studying for a BSc in Anatomy. Kevin was therefore eighteen months ahead of us and qualified as a medical doctor that length of time before us. The friendship between Colin and me was a close one. We were in digs together for the first term, and then later, in a flat together with some of my UCL friends.

After the three of us had qualified and married, Felicity and I maintained contact with Colin and Ann but there was less contact with Kevin and Shelagh. Ann was a nurse at the London Hospital. Shelagh was a fellow medical student who became a GP. Colin and Ann settled near Tavistock in Devon. He was then a consultant breast surgeon. Kevin and Shelagh settled in Lancashire. Kath and I mainly saw Colin and Ann at a reunion of about twenty people who meet annually. We also met Kevin and Shelagh there but, in later years, got together more often both in our main houses and occasionally in the second home Kath and I had in Swaledale.

Kevin and Shelagh are great walkers. A coincidence occurred in the Yorkshire Dales. Kath and I were on a walk, and we met Kevin and Shelagh. We did not know they were in the Dales. They were on a completely different walk from ours. Our walks overlapped for only about a quarter of a mile. There is where we met. We had a pub lunch together.

Kath and I visited London as often as we could. We loved the city. We bumped into Colin and Ann on two occasions. We did not know they were in town. Once was in the Drury Lane Moat House Hotel and the other was in the Barbican concert hall. Coincidences?

Colin developed multiple sclerosis, which progressed slowly. There was one weekend when both couples came to Yorkshire. I organised a private trip round our school and a retired history master was our tour guide. We also went to the Hepworth art gallery and the Yorkshire Sculpture Park. Colin had to stay in a hotel because of his disability. I think he knew he would not be coming up to Yorkshire again.

From 2021 Colin's health significantly deteriorated. That year we held the reunion near their house in Devon. Ann was an angel in how she cared for him. They joined us for one evening meal and the next morning we all went to the house and enjoyed a drink in their lovely garden.

Diana Shalet, Kevin, and Colin

The venue of the reunion was repeated in October 2022. Prior to that, Colin had several admissions with inhalation pneumonia and was expected not to survive on at least two occasions. He said goodbye to Eric, his brother, on one of those occasions. We could not meet Colin at all that second time because he was again in hospital with limited visiting. He died at home in April 2023. I went to his memorial service in Tavistock, which was packed. Robin gave a lovely eulogy. I will never forget the big man-hug we gave one another when we met. May Colin rest in peace.

I met Kevin and Shelagh for lunch at the Trafford Centre in May 2023. They were upset to miss Colin's funeral because of a holiday. For me to have Colin and Kevin as friends at school, university, and later in my life gives me such a warm feeling and a realisation of how lucky I am.

So, after University College London I started at the London Hospital Medical College to undertake clinical training. That involved all sorts of disciplines we had to know about – skin diseases, surgery, maternity, psychiatry, general medicine, medication, cardiology, and more besides. It was mind blowing to me. On top of that, learning how to talk to and examine patients. I made more friends at The London.

There were four of us who had undertaken the BSc in Anatomy: Colin (mentioned above), Adrian Bomford, Robin Harrod, and me. Three of us were from the north. Adrian had a southern accent and the other three of us, Yorkshire accents. We were in the same tutorial group together and were told that we should take elocution lessons, or we would never get anywhere in medicine. We took no notice. After all, it was the 1960s.

Robin and Christine Harrod

During the three years of clinical training, Robin and I made good friends, and he started going out with Christine, a dental student. I was going out first with Kath and then Felicity, a medical student at St. Mary's Hospital Medical School. Robin was my best man at my and Felicity's wedding.

Robin and me at my first wedding   Robin at a reunion

There have been several amazing acts of friendship towards me from Robin and Christine. After being my best man, Robin told me of a vacancy for a partner in his general practice in Cheltenham. I was approaching the end of my three-year stint as a lecturer in physiology in London. I had always intended to become a GP. I had an interview at the practice, and they offered me a partnership. That was an amazing act of friendship. Cheltenham was a very attractive town and Felicity and I bought a townhouse quite near where Robin and Christine lived. Felicity took up a paediatrics job in Cheltenham followed by a partnership in a GP practice in town. The friendship between the Harrods and us strengthened and the professional relationship between Robin and me was excellent. They had three children, all girls: Samantha, Joanna, and Alexandra. Another big act of friendship was that they asked Felicity to be godmother of Joanna, and me, godfather of Samantha. I was honoured, but very anxious, to be asked to say something at Samantha's twenty-first birthday celebration and to read a poem at her wedding. Samantha and I are Facebook friends.

Samantha

I let Robin down when Felicity and I split up. I resigned the partnership he had set up for me, and the practice had to pay out my share of the building. I left town. I am sure Robin felt let down and that it affected his and Christine's friendship with me. I was feeling stressed and bereaved. I could have handled the situation better. Old friendships rarely die. We are still firm friends. There was a period, in Cheltenham, when I was living alone and still working as a GP. Another act of great kindness from Robin and Chris was to invite me to stay with them and celebrate Christmas with their family. I had the greatest of difficulty in Castleford obtaining locum cover for holidays. Robin arranged that a trainee doctor could cover for me if he was supervised by my retired mother! I think we would have all been struck off doing something like that these days. Kath and I and Robin and Chris often stayed at one another's houses. One memorable time was when the whole family came up and stayed the weekend of the Live Aid concert (Saturday 13 July 1985). Robin and Chris came up for Kath's funeral in 2015. He was my best man again at that event, particularly the evening before.

We have not kept in touch as much as in the past, but when we do meet, this old and firm friendship with Robin and Christine is rekindled.

Gill Kavanagh and the late Wendy Knighton

Gill and Wendy at my and Kath's wedding, 1978

Gill and Wendy were flatmates with Kath in 1977 at 47 Harrington Gardens, Kensington. I met them when Kath and I got together again. They continued as close friends of Kath, and I was so pleased that they included me.

Wendy was one of the most vivacious people I have ever met and was expert at making me blush with embarrassment. She had a very loud voice. When we met her in London, her greeting was overwhelming and included screaming with joy and big hugs. At one point, she had an Egyptian boyfriend, Ragi Saba. Ragi lived in England for several years and moved back to Egypt and married Hodi. He is a successful businessman. They both came over to the UK sometime before Kath died, and we went out for a meal with them and Gill. I have kept in touch with Ragi. Wendy had a relationship with Amir, and they had a daughter, Amy. Wendy was involved in two car crashes. The first was many years ago in Scotland, when she was significantly injured, but not as bad as a second car accident later in her life. That event caused brain damage and she spent the rest of her life wheelchair-bound in a care home. Wendy died, aged 66, in 2017.

Gill was a fantastic friend to Kath and me and she has continued as a great friend with me after Kath's death. She has a wonderful sense of humour. We used to meet her and Wendy when we came to London and they both used to come and stay with us. They stayed at our main home and sometimes at the second home in Gunnerside, Swaledale. Gill bought a ground-floor flat in the Notting Hill area of London. Some years later she bought the upstairs flat. Gill made the property into a very comfortable terraced house with two bedrooms. She used to call the spare bedroom "The Sloan Suite". David Cameron owned a house in the next street while he was the leader of the Conservative Party. The area was often buzzing with press. Gill used to say that she put make-up on when she was going to the dustbin just in case she was caught in a photograph! I never met her mother, but her father was also great fun. He started as a constable policeman in Liverpool and retired as the deputy commissioner of the Metropolitan Police.

Patrick Kavanagh CBE (Paddy)

When we were staying at Gill's on a Sunday, she would invite him for Sunday lunch. It was a very pleasant experience. He lived in Epsom, and we once met him at his house, and then went on to Woodcote Park, which is a stately home owned by the Royal Automobile Club. He was a little unsteady on his feet and rested his hand on my shoulder as we walked from the car to the house. I felt I was being arrested.

Gill has lots of friends in London and one is Linda Parker, who also lives alone since the death of her husband. Linda is a very lively person and great fun. We once met her in Italy when she was staying with an architect friend near our home in Umbria. Gill used to choose the restaurant where we ate in London. Sometimes Linda came with us. Both worked for the BBC. Gill was involved with *The Money Programme*. Linda was involved with a documentary on India and did some work with Richard Attenborough, who directed the film *Gandhi*. Gill's father died at the age of 90 in 2013, and we went to his funeral. He had a full-page obituary in *The Times*. He was in charge of the police response to the siege on the Iranian Embassy in 1980.

These days, I meet Gill as often as I can when I am in London, usually for a meal in the evening. She gets on with anybody and has joined me and different friends of mine to dine out. She once said that her favourite meal was the leftovers! When she is in France with one of her friends and they run out of leftovers, they go out and buy some more!

Desert Island Discs

In the mid-1980s, Shelagh Taylor worked for the Area Health Authority. She was an ex-health visitor and spent some time at the London Hospital, where I was, in the 1970s. Our general practice decided to undertake the King's Fund Organisational Audit. This was a major exercise of policy and procedure writing and the facilitator was Shelagh. Kath was the practice manager and we got to know Shelagh very well, and that is how we became friends. She and her husband, Paul, introduced us to some of their friends. We started socialising together: meals at one another's houses, supporting the Castleford Choral Society as patrons, and eventually we were a group of eight who met four times a year to listen to music. We called the evening Desert Island Discs. We had a buffet meal halfway through the music. Shelagh's husband, Paul, was a retired science teacher. The other members of the group were George Gauden (his wife died some time before the music group was created), Sue Northcote (her husband died years before), Pam Hesseltine and John Griffiths, Kath and me. We met together in this group for about twenty years. We each brought two tracks to play and tell a narrative as to the reason for the choice. Some of the group could be described as talented musicians. I can play the piano by ear, but it is very simple stuff and is not a talent.

John was the conductor of Castleford Choral Society for seventeen years and composed. His partner, Pam, plays the cello and was a significant soprano and a member of several choirs. Kath played the piano very well and took up the church organ in the latter part of her life. She sang as an alto in the Leeds Philharmonic Choir. Paul also composed. One of his compositions was premiered in the Castleford Civic Centre by Willard White, the famous bass-baritone. It was a unique group of friends. During recent years Kath, George, Sue, and Shelagh have died and we no longer meet as a group. Pam, John, and Paul continue as my friends.

Liz Wheeldon nee Box

Those of you who haven't fallen asleep reading this chapter might have noticed that Liz's surname is the same as Rosslynne's (see above) maiden name. Liz married Rosslynne's brother, William. The Box family is large and had a close relationship with my family from being patients. William died relatively young a long time ago. Liz has lived alone for many years. One of Liz's three brothers, Peter, is a friend of mine from when we were young and attending the same school. Peter and I are fellow trustees of a small charity, Spectrum People. He was leader of Wakefield Council for twenty-eight years.

Peter Box, 2023

Liz's aunt, Edna Box, was the midwife at my parent's general practice. Edna was a wonderful person. That branch of the Box family also had a friendship relationship with my parents. Indeed, after my father died, and Edna had retired, my mother and she became firm friends and went on holidays together. I have written about Edna at some length in my last book entitled *Tieve Tara*.

When Rosslynne and John visited Airedale in later years, we would invite Liz either for a coffee or a meal.

Liz's father, George, was a barber. I think he also dealt with women's hair. Liz used to work with him. George cut my hair when I was 4 years old. He once came to our house when my father was not well and cut his hair in the garden as it was a lovely day! When George retired, Liz took over.

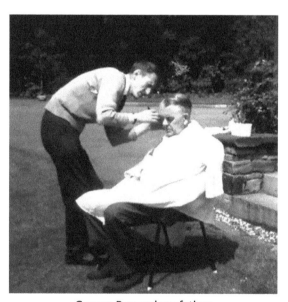

George Box and my father

I went to George Box, and then Liz, from 1978 until Liz retired in 2000.

Liz came to Kath's funeral. I thought that was a very kind thing to do and our good friendship continued.

We have a completely different tastes in music, but both appreciate art. She is very knowledgeable about local artists and writers and enjoys modern art and sculpture. Her brother, Peter, was a major player in the building of the new Hepworth Gallery in Wakefield. Liz and I go out for lunches, both locally and further afield in Yorkshire. She is very good at talking to strangers, and I have learnt a few things about that skill from her! However, talking to strangers does not always go smoothly. I went to a theatre matinee in London. A couple were sitting next to me. After the interval, the husband went off to buy an ice cream for his wife. When he got back, I said "I hope you don't mind me talking to your wife." He replied, "How do you know she's my wife?" I am convinced it was his wife!

Liz and I go to London together quite a lot. One can easily go for the day using the train from Wakefield. For a reason that is beyond me, Liz does not like having her photograph taken. However, she has allowed me to use the one below.

Liz Wheeldon at Gisborough Hall

One of the reasons we go to London is to meet a mutual friend, Christopher Smith. We both knew him when we were younger. When I describe the friendship that has developed between the three of us, readers might conclude that this could be a case study of friendships. Old, close, good, loving, family, impossible, rekindled, lifelong and ex-friendships.

I have mentioned how different our tastes are in music. Let me tell you of another difference. Liz has a collection of bricks, and I have a collection of handbags! She is a great mother of two boys, and she idolises her four grandchildren.

One of our similarities is we undertake voluntary work helping people much less fortunate than ourselves. She regularly works for the charity the Pontefract Community Kitchen and I for the charity Spectrum People.

Christopher J. F. Smith

Christopher James Fox Smith. Lunch at the RSM, 2015

After Kath died, I tried to rekindle old friendships. Some of those meetings worked, but others did not. It was good to have a meeting with an old friend, but I think those that did not work ended up as just a catch-up one-off meal. Friendships end just as marriages can end. I did not "click" with one or two of my friends from the past. The feeling was obviously mutual.

One of the meetings that did work was with Christopher Smith. Christopher's parents, Maurice and Muriel, were friends of my parents. Maurice was my parents' solicitor. Chris is a little older than I am. We become close friends when we were both at the junior school of Queen Elizabeth Grammar School, Wakefield. Chris went on from there to Rossall School at Fleetwood, Lancashire. We remained friends. We kept in touch during university holidays (Chris went to Bristol University). He studied law. We also met in London occasionally when he came across from Bristol at the weekends. Gradually, we lost touch, even though he worked as a partner in his father's firm in Castleford for a while. I did hear a little about him from my mother, who kept in touch with the Smiths after my father died.

Then I arranged to meet Christopher in the Royal Society of Medicine (RSM) for lunch. I went to London on my own. We had not met for decades. I was upset at first that he did not recognise me. I recognised him but it took a few seconds. The memory system of the human brain is complex. We obviously clicked. Christopher emailed me to say that we had only got through 35% of the catch-up and must meet again.

So, what is the connection between Christopher and Liz Wheeldon?

It was when Christopher was working in Castleford that he and Liz became a serious item. They became engaged. The engagement did not work out. She later married William Wheeldon.

As I mentioned above, Liz and I started to go to London together with the main objective being to meet Chris and his wife, Caroline. Liz met up with Chris and Caroline years ago and the three have a very amicable relationship. Chris and Caroline are the most amazing parents with a wonderful marriage. They have two daughters, Georgia and Martha. Georgia is severely disabled. Their lovely house in Islington has many adaptations. Like Jennifer and Tom, above, Chris and Caroline's life revolves around Georgia.

After Liz and I met them in a pub in Yorkshire in 2023, we were saying goodbye in the car park. Liz went to her car to get a present she had bought for the Smiths. Two bricks! Brick collecting is as serious as stamp collecting. Bricks have markings, history, etc. Perhaps the next time we meet Chris, I will give him a handbag.

More friends made since 1978

Kath and I were married in 1978, and later that year, on impulse, moved into the empty house my mother owned and where I was brought up. We set up a general practice from scratch in the surgery, which was semi-detached from the private house. Kath had friends she had known literally all her life. In time, would I make friends with them? I certainly made friends with friends of my first wife, Felicity, and vice versa. Indeed, she is now a close friend of Robin Harrod, who was my best man at our wedding (see earlier).

Kath and Alan Overton

Kath and Alan came from the same village (Woodford Halse, Northamptonshire) as my late wife, Kath. Their parents were friends. Kath S was a bridesmaid for Kath O at her wedding. The two Kaths went to the same school. I realised something about friendship when Kath and Alan invited us to their wedding anniversary celebration. My Kath knew all of them, I think. I was a bit worried that I would be out of it. It was not a huge group of people and we all sat on the same table for a lovely meal. I realised that the saying "any friend of yours is a friend of mine" had a large element of truth in it. After a very short while, I knew I could get on with each of them. My Kath and I, Kath and Alan, and two of those friends, Ann and Paul, went on holidays to Israel and Italy. After Kath died, in 2017 the five of us went to Opatija, Croatia together and Italy once more. Malcolm and Beryl, other friends of the two Kaths and Alan, joined us in Italy a couple of times, but stayed in a lovely hotel situated on the shores of Lake Trasimeno.

We four had the same wedding anniversary month and day, 3 June.

Alan, Kath S, Kath O, and me, 3 June 2014
Bagno Vignoni Roman Baths, Tuscany

We spent Christmases together, and in the early days that included their two children, Jane and Richard. Jane was one of my Kath's goddaughters and she had a very soft spot for her. Since Kath's death, I have adopted Jane (unofficially) as one of my goddaughters. Jane was very fond of our first labrador dog, Sindy. Sindy got upset when Jane left our house after a stay. Jane has a gentle and quiet personality. When Richard was 9 years old, he wrote a letter of complaint to the council at York. He complained about the fact we had paid to enter to a public gents and I was sprayed with cold water from a defective sink tap.

The four adults went on many holidays together. We went away somewhere at least once a year and we used our second home in Gunnerside, Swaledale, frequently. We went to the USA several times, and Italy many times. We stayed in the house Kath and I owned in Umbria, Italy.

Our friendship has not faltered since Kath's death. I think it has strengthened. Jane has a lovely daughter, Georgia, who has just

(2023) obtained a good degree in Psychology. Richard has a senior job at the Halifax bank and he and his wife, Anna, settled in Wakefield, which is only about 10 miles from me. He and Anna have two children. Daniel is a radiographer in Leeds and Jacob will be going to university soon.

Both Kath and Alan have had significant illnesses in very recent years. We keep in touch very regularly using Facetime, etc. We had a wonderful holiday in September 2023. Eight nights on a Saga cruise ship travelling around the British Isles with stops.

How could I describe my friendship with Kath and Alan? Close, remarkable, steady, understanding, tolerant, fortunate.

Jane and me, *Queen Mary 2*, 2023

Martin and Jennifer (Jen) Smith, and Stephen and Averil Smith

Martin (see chapter 2) is a relation of Kath's and, therefore, indirectly of me. He is the grandson of Kath's father (Charlie) from the first marriage. That first marriage resulted in one child, Mabel. Mabel was Martin's mother. Her husband, Sidney, was his father. Kath and I saw them often. Martin is only slightly younger than me. Martin and Jen live in Leeds. Before we could move into Tieve Tara in Castleford, we stayed in a hotel north of Leeds to be able to visit Martin, Jen and the two children, Claire and Nigel.

We had many Christmases together either in our house or theirs. We went on many holidays together – France, Italy, and weekend breaks with Martin's brother, Steven, and his wife, Averil, to places like Brussels, Lisbon, Barcelona, and more. They stayed at our house in Macchie, Italy and we spent time with them at their lovely house in Somerset. Martin's brother was, like me, a medical student at the London Hospital. Averil was a nurse at The London. Stephen and Averil are a bit younger than me. The six of us had great fun together. Kath and I also had wonderful times and fun with the children of these families. Stephen and Averil have two children, Philip and Joanna.

Left to right: Martin, Stephen, Averil, and Jen

The day Kath died in hospital, I telephoned Martin and Jen, and, without hesitation, they came over from Leeds, and went up the road and bought fish and chips. I will never forget Jen offering me an arm to lean on at the end of Kath's funeral, as we made our way out of the church. Both Martin and Kath Overton read at Kath's funeral. My friendship with the Smith family is set in concrete.

I have enjoyed seeing the children of the two families grow up. I will not go into details only to inform you that by the time this book is published, Claire, Nigel and I will have been married seven times between us.

Claire was a goddaughter of my Kath and since her death I have, like with Jane, also unofficially adopted her as my goddaughter. Claire and I have exchanged texts nearly every day since Kath died over eight years ago. We have done things together. She is a very kind person. She and John, her husband, live in Bath and have three sons, Alfie, Ewan, and William.

Claire and me

The Smith families are blood relations of Kath. The members of the two families have known one another closely since they were children. I have got similar genetic relations with whom I keep in touch, and we have known one another since we were children. I will refrain from writing about them just as I have not written about Kath and Felicity. I am looking at non-family friendships in the main.

Bill and Anna Bullingham

Bill and Anna made Felicity and me very welcome when we arrived in Cheltenham. Bill was a patient of my general practice. They invited us to dinner parties, and we met people through these events, some of whom became friends. Some were also friends of Robin and Chris: Mike and Sue Hare, Penny and Nick Stones, Tim and Pat Powell, Liz and Roger Williams.

Bill is a very successful property developer like his father before him. His partner now is their eldest son, Simon. He and Anna were wealthy and generous with their friends. I was only in Cheltenham for four years. We bought a three-storey townhouse to start with. It was in a block of new townhouses, so everyone who bought one of these were new neighbours. That was a great catalyst for developing friendships. Next door were David and Ute Stevens. David was a consultant neurologist just starting at Gloucester Royal Infirmary. Felicity and I made good friends with them, and I see them occasionally when I visit Cheltenham. I am sure that buying a newly built house is a great asset for building up friendships.

We were not in that house for long when Bill tipped us off about a bungalow in one of the poshest areas of Cheltenham called Battledown. There was a rumour that it had something seriously wrong with the roof. Because of that, we got it relatively cheaply. We were not in that place for long when Bill found another bargain. We sold the Battledown house after spending about £100 on the roof! The last house in Cheltenham was a magnificent building in Tivoli Road built sometime in the 1800s. It sold well when Felicity and I broke up.

35 Tivoli Road 2023

The photographs above are from an estate agent's website (2/10/23). The asking price is £2.2 m.

When I remarried, it was a great act of friendship that Bill and Anna befriended Kath with open arms.

Bill and Anna had four children, three boys and a girl. I was honoured (like with Robin and Chris) to be asked to be godfather to Rachael, their daughter.

Rachael Bullingham

Rachael is a great goddaughter and I love meeting her. I was proud when she obtained a PhD. I have a godson in Australia,

Nicholas Earls, who is a successful author, and who was relatively recently awarded a PhD. Like me, he is also a medical doctor. Rachael is happily married to Josie, and not only do I enjoy meeting them, but also following Rachael, who is a Facebook friend. They are such good fun.

The boys (Simon, Mark, and Jo) have each been so friendly with us for all these years. We visited one another and they stayed with us in the Gunnerside house. I must quote something one of the boys said when we were walking across a field near the Swaledale house. Mark was a quiet person. He had not said much for ages. He suddenly looked down and said, "Nothing but shit and dead rabbits!" Mark Bullingham is now chief executive of the Football Association. I think he might get a knighthood. Joe is a lovable rogue, and I really get on with him as did Kath. Simon is married to a doctor, and they have a lovely family.

We had a couple of very memorable holidays together. A gang of us went to an international rugby match in Paris for the weekend. It was a great experience and great fun.

In the early 1980s nineteen of us, including children, went to Barbados for New Year. Bill and Anna flew first class. Kath and I were in second class smoking. I think we had to get permission from the captain to visit Bill and Anna on the flight! It was a fantastic holiday, and we were knocking back champagne at about £40 a bottle (£135 in today's money). We had two Mini Mokes which we shared. We put all the drinks on the account of one of the children's rooms, Room 73. The children cottoned onto this, and we found a lot of ice cream on that bill at the end. We shared the bill for Room 73 between the adults. I will not publish how much that bill was for each couple, but we did not begrudge a penny.

It was on the beach in front of the hotel where I saw the green flash. I knew about it before the trip. What is the green flash? It happens when the sun is almost entirely below the horizon, with the barest edge of the sun – the upper edge – still visible. For a second or two, that upper rim of the sun will appear green in colour. It is rarely seen and brief. I saw it. On two or three consecutive evenings, I insisted on my friends coming out to see it. None of them did. I saw it. They decided I had a screw loose. When I got home, I wrote to Patrick Moore, the astronomer, and asked if he would kindly confirm the existence of the green flash in a letter to me, so I could show my friends. He did indeed send me a postcard with the confirmation.

The green flash

Bill and Anna's marriage broke up, and after that, we lost touch with Bill, which I regret. We kept in touch with Anna. The reason we lost touch with Bill that we took Anna's "side". However, Bill came to Kath's funeral in 2015 with Joe, and Anna came with Rachael, which was another great act of friendship. Soon after Kath's death, Bill phoned me and asked if I would like to go with him to a fundraising event for Bowel and Cancer Research. This is a charity founded in about 2006 and the president was Sir Norman Williams. Bill was the founder director. (Norman Williams was at the London Hospital at the same time as me. He became the President of the Royal College of Surgeons. Kath and I met him when we were staying with Bill and Anna. He wrote to me after Kath died and wrote a paragraph for me to read at my friend Mike Dawson's memorial event.) I contacted Anna and asked her if she would mind if I went to the event with Bill. I did not want it to affect our friendship. She had been brilliant with me when I was so upset about my own marriage breaking down.

She told me she thought I would enjoy the event. I did. It was a dinner with very expensive raffle tickets and an auction which raised thousands of pounds. Another act of friendship was that Simon came from Cheltenham to London especially to see me and sat next to me. Bill resigned as a director of the charity in 2019. I think it merged with another company, but it is still the major bowel charity of the UK, 'Bowel Cancer UK'.

I was invited to Anna's second marriage to Peter. I have stayed with them since in Salcombe. I have also stayed with Bill and Tanya, his long-standing partner. She is a very kind Ukrainian. They helped a lot of relations at the start of the war between Ukraine and Russia.

Friendships are strained with both marriage breakdowns and deaths. This is a well-documented situation, which I have experienced personally. I have mentioned above my blocking out of Bill. In retrospect, that was a mistake. Anna has maintained her friendship with me since the friendship between Bill and me was restored. She is a good friend of my first wife, Felicity, as are Robin and Christine Harrod. I am sure It is very difficult to remain even-handed friends of each of a couple who have split up.

When two couples meet for the first time and develop a friendship bond, is the strength of the bond that develops the same between any two of the four? That can include two who are a couple. I mentioned friendship within marriage in the early part of this chapter. The relationship of friendship within my marriage to Kath was crucial. This is often an underestimated aspect of a successful and fulfilling partnership.

Readers will have their own opinions about friendship. I have described mine. However, a book that was recommended to me by Anna Hartley, the recent director of Public Health, Wakefield, gave me great food for thought. Anna and I were always friendly towards one another when we met, which was always professionally. I highly respect her and her work.

*Friendaholic – confessions of a friendship addict by Elizabeth Day. 4*th *Estate – London. 2023.*

I played squash regularly with the late Chris Bullingham, Bill's brother. After I left Cheltenham and moved up to Castleford, I received a Christmas card every year for many years. It was signed "Floss and Val". I had no idea who they were. I found out in the end. They were Bill and Chris's mother and sister, respectively.

I also played squash with Mike Hare. He and Sue lived up the road from us in The Park.

Tim Powell was an insurance broker married to Pat. They were in the gang that went to Barbados. Tieve Tara surgery used Tim for professional advice for years. There were others that were friends of both of us.

When my marriage to Felicity ended, I decided I would leave Cheltenham. I held a leaving party (1973). I invited friends and colleagues from far and wide. At the bottom of the invitation card, it stated "Please wear a false nose".

Here are photos of some of the guests.

Me

David Stevens, consultant neurologist

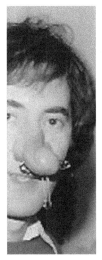

Dr. Jeff Marks, consultant psychiatrist

Mike Hare, builder (Concorde nose)

Richard Baker, partner (now, professor emeritus, Leicester)

Dr. Tony Mules, GP, senior partner

There was roulette and Tim Powell was the table croupier. He wore a green eye shade. Profits went to charity. What I forgot until halfway through the evening was that I could have lost money!

The Reunion

A small group of friends who met at the London Hospital at the start of our clinical studies in 1966 have held an annual reunion for decades. None of us can remember exactly when we started. There is a firm record of a reunion in 1973. We had reunions before that. The friends are accompanied by their wives. In the case of three couples, all six attended the medical or nursing school.

The reunions took place mainly in the UK but we have also been abroad – France, Italy, and the USA. One year, in the early days, we rented a house and had students cook for us. Another year, we hired a long boat. We take it in turns to organise the reunions – this is about every ten years. Spouses have changed. Members have died. For a significant number of years now, we have been going to smart hotels with our own private dining room.

I have mentioned some of the group above: Robin and Chris, Brian and Kate, Colin and Anne, Kevin and Shelagh, Steve, and Diana. We all know one another well. I would say we are very good friends who enjoy one another's company and conversation. I feel I could telephone anyone of the group if I was in any trouble or distressed.

Okehampton, the private dining room

We used this venue because it was close to where Colin and Ann lived. They came to this meal for a short time. Colin could not find a hotel in the UK that could cope with his level of disability. The next day we were invited to their house for drinks.

He was so strong and was looked after by an angel, Ann. She trained as a nurse at the London Hospital. Colin fought on and nearly died a couple of times in 2022. We came again to Okehampton in October that year to be near him and Ann. We could not see him. He was admitted to hospital with aspiration pneumonia secondary to his swallowing deteriorating. We did see Ann after the second meal, however. Robin and Christine were fantastic in supporting Colin and Ann throughout his illness.

There is more to friendship than just getting together for a couple of meals in a posh hotel. This is a unique group of friends.

Some of the group could not make the trip to the USA. Mike Dawson became a distinguished orthopaedic surgeon in Pottsville, Pennsylvania, and organised a reunion in Philadelphia. I have written about him and Pauline extensively in my book *The English Doctor*, published in 2012. Mike was my bridge and sometimes boozing partner at The London. Before surgery took place at the

London Hospital, the day before, a male patient had to be shaved from the nipples to the knees. Mike and I shared this job, which involved each of us shaving the lateral half of what was required. We raced one another. The loser had to buy a pint of beer for the other. I wonder what the patient thought. Pauline gave me the honour of asking me to say a few words at Mike's memorial event held at the Royal College of Surgeons in London at the end of October 2021. Mike and Pauline owned a house south of the river in London. It was good to meet them there occasionally and sample Pauline's excellent Malaysian cuisine.

Philadelphia, 2006. L to R, Back: Kate, Brian, Robin, Kevin, Shelagh, me, Mike
Front: Christine, Kath, Pauline, Ann, Colin

During the reunion in Philadelphia, we went on an excursion in a duck boat on the Delaware River. A duck boat is an amphibious vehicle. We were each issued with a small yellow instrument which produced a quacking sound when blown. You can see in the photo that on the back row, Professor Colvin is quacking enthusiastically. After one of the most expensive meals I have ever had, we walked to a viewpoint at the top of a skyscraper. Mike walked ahead. Unfortunately, we got stuck in the lift for quite a while until we were rescued. Mike was relaxing with a beer at the bar.

There were two reunions in the residence of the British ambassador to the Holy See, situated on the outskirts of Rome. Kathryn Colvin was the ambassador to the Holy See. Kath and I only made one of those, but it was a fantastic experience. Kate had five members of staff to look after her. Chauffeur, chef, gardener and two more. After one of the evening meals, three of us had a go on the piano – Kath, me, and Mike. Kath was a very good pianist, as was Mike. I play by ear, and I think I played items like "It's a long way to Tipperary" and "Colonel Bogey". Look at the photos on the piano. There is one of Kate with Pope John Paul II.

Rome, 2004

It was a wonderful experience, and we had a private tour of the basement of the Vatican as well as the gardens.

With Steve Shalet, I am organising the 2023 reunion, which is at Gisborough Hall, North Yorkshire. 2023 is sixty years since we all started as medical students at the London Hospital Medical College, Cambridge, or in my case, University College London. It is fifty-seven years since we all started clinical studies together.

In the same week as the London Hospital mini reunion described above, there is the sixtieth anniversary of my becoming a medical student at University College London in 1963. I was there for three years. I went to the last reunion, which was in 2018.

UCL Reunion 2018, Grahame and Steve

We are standing in front of a noticeboard which has photographs of all those who have died. Three of my friends are in that photograph: Jim Smeeton, Abdul Paliwala and Geoff Mair.

Abdul

Abdul

Abdul developed a form of Parkinson's disease after heart surgery. I went to his first wedding. He was born and brought up in Zanzibar. Some of our friends visited there for holidays. As his illness progressed,

Grahame, Steve and I visited him for the day where he lived in North London. Colin Parker joined us a couple of times. We went out for lunch and afterwards he showed us his recent art works. He was a talented artist. Grahame and I went to his Muslim funeral.

Geoff and Zoe

Geoff. From BMJ Obituary

Geoff and Zoe were good friends of Kath and me. Geoff went to school with Steve Haggie and was a fellow biker with Grahame. They went all over Europe on frightening-looking and powerful motorbikes. Kath and I exchanged Christmas cards with Geoff and Zoe for several years. I always wrote in the card "we are on the way". Eventually, we met at one another's houses every year. Geoff developed a serious lung disease with increasing breathlessness, which required portable oxygen. We spent a weekend with Geoff and Zoe in London and one in Venice, when he was on the oxygen. The Venice trip was shortly after he retired. Geoff commented, "I think this is the daftest place to go to if you can't breathe." We decided we could only afford one of the three evenings having a postprandial drink and a coffee in St Mark's Square. We went there every night. Life is precious. Geoff and Zoe were great fun. They came to my fiftieth birthday party at our house in Airedale. They brought what looked like an iced birthday cake. An announcement was made that the cake would be cut outside. The cake was a huge firework, which was magnificent. In the end, Geoff had a heart/lung transplant. He died not a very long time after that. I had the honour of being asked to write his obituary for the *British Medical Journal*.

Airedale, Castleford from 1978

I have written about friends John Lee (GP partner), Anne Godridge (GP partner), Sue Smith (health visitor) and other friends in my book, *Tieve Tara*. I have written about old friendships which have strengthened since I came to be a GP in Castleford. What about new friends?

Kath and I had a driver who took us to social events. There were two of them while Kath was alive. We therefore rarely used taxis. I wrote about Kevin Tansley and Derek Turner in the book *Tieve Tara*. Derek was the first but had to give up because of ill health. Each of these men were so reliable but also kind. Derek had been in the army and Kevin was a coal miner. Kevin died some short time after Kath. George now drives me.

I thought of dedicating this book to the late Norman Batty. The reason for that is I feel very guilty that I forgot to mention Norman in the *Tieve Tara* book. He looked after the house and dog when we were away. He took our dog to his home, where he lived with his partner, Gloria.

Norman Batty and Gloria West

Gloria had poor health and was on oxygen for quite a time before she died. Norman was a bit of a practical joker and wrote poetry. I never quite believed some of the things he told me. For example, he said he had had all his teeth extracted to stop him biting his nails. The other thing he told me was that he was good with animals because he once had a job mucking out the elephants in Billy Smart's circus. Norman was a retired coal miner. Gloria's lung problem deteriorated to such an extent that she became housebound. Norman carried on helping us, and at the same time looked after Gloria like gold. Of course, I informed them about Kath's funeral in 2015. They could not come because Gloria was housebound. However, when I emerged from the church after the funeral, there they were sitting in the car very close to the front of the church. Gloria was on her oxygen. I was overwhelmed with this act of friendship and loyalty. They told me they just wanted to pay their respects. Norman was somewhat in love with Kath. He was devastated when Gloria died. He read one of his poems at her funeral. Norman died suddenly. I went to his funeral in Airedale Methodist Church. There was a packed congregation that included many ex-coal miners. These strong and tough men were sobbing at one point. The camaraderie and friendship between male coal miner friends is very strong.

Neighbours

I have the most fantastic neighbours here in Airedale Drive. I am hopeless with do-it-yourself or repairing anything. I regard Ronnie and Evelyn as close friends. We will do anything for one another. Over the years, Ronnie has helped me with all sorts of tasks in the house and with the car.

Ronnie and Evelyn Smith

They had a very neurologically challenged daughter, Vicky. They looked after her so well. Vicky died from an accident not long ago and this has been a big loss for them. I have never seen such caring parents. For several years now, Evelyn and I have exchanged a Facebook message every day with snippets of news and to say how we are. Ronnie has two garages where he has hoarded all sorts of things over many years. I once went round because the paper was stuck in my printer. He went into one of these garages and found a pair of surgical forceps, which did the trick! Evelyn was a particular friend of Kath's and they used to go shopping together. They also went to the Conservative Luncheon Club. Kath thought her father would turn in his grave. He was a serious Labour Party member and union man.

The other neighbours are:

Dick – his wife, Jessie, died not so long ago. He lives alone and has a good family nearby. He is blind.

Dave and Janet – they know many local people and would do anything to help.

Ken and Beryl – they moved from the south of England. Ken has poor mobility and Beryl now does the driving.

Louise and Julian – younger than me.

David and family– David, like me, was brought up in his house.

Tieve Tara Medical Centre

I have written about the colleagues I worked with when I was a GP in my book *Tieve Tara*. My mother believed that a general practice medical partnership was like a marriage. For many years, we were three partners – John Lee, Anne Godridge, and me. I feel John is my friend. We mainly communicate these days using Facebook. Anne retired and it is great that we are both members of the Castleford Singers. That means we see one another at the weekly rehearsals. I am not sure whether Anne will agree with this. She had two periods of maternity leave. That is sometimes difficult for the remaining two equity partners of a small business like a general practice. I was pleased that she had a family. Her mother, Mrs. Whitehouse, helped us out as a temporary secretary at one point. My career developed in such a way that I had outside work for the postgraduate education world. I always felt grateful to Anne for agreeing to my absence from the general practice to undertake the role of an education. Of course, John also agreed. He helped me a lot to become a GP trainer. John moved away from general practice a long time ago and had a fulfilled hospital-based career. I feel that Anne and I are good friends. The day before writing this (13 September 2023), I attended the funeral of Tom, the 27-year-old son of Alan and Anne. He died from Cardiac Risk in the Young. It was undiagnosed and sudden. It was the biggest funeral I have attended. The presence of so many rctired and working members of staff from Tieve Tara Medical Centre was not only a mark of respect, but also an act of friendship. When I talk to other general practitioners, I know that the friendly relationship between all who worked at the surgery was unique, both when I was senior partner and then with Anne in the same role.

Castleford Singers, previously known as The Castleford Choral Society

This is a very friendly choir. Kath joined round about 1980 and I, sometime after that. Maureen, our housekeeper, also joined. We took her to choir and back every Wednesday evening when there was a rehearsal. The choir was founded by Lily Travis in 1932. She was my first piano teacher. The choir has been going for over ninety years now. Kath was the secretary for many years and, up to the time of writing, I have been the patrons' secretary for twenty-two years. Maureen served the tea and coffee at the interval. I searched through many photographs of the choir, going back decades, to decide which one to include in this chapter. Mrs. Wheeldon, the president of the Castleford Choral Society, as it was previously called, always made a speech after a concert. The photo is of Kath presenting her with flowers. It shows two smiling friends.

Kath and our president, Mrs. May Wheeldon

I have mentioned Mrs. Wheeldon at the start of this chapter when writing about our friend and her daughter, Rosslynne. Before making the big move to Castleford in 1978, I had asked advice from Mrs. Wheeldon. She became a firm friend of both of us and helped us by suggesting to her friends that they became my patients. She had a great number of contacts and was a JP. She was an active president and was responsible for recruiting many of the patrons. (My father was a patron in the 1950s.) She persuaded me to stand for the position of chair of the choir committee. It was a bit of a coup and some of the members of the choir were upset that I ousted the then chairman, Harold Firth. I was the chair for ten years and Kath, the secretary for even more years. Mrs. Wheeldon was looking after us and wanted us to succeed. She got on well with my mother and particularly my father. My mother thought she was somewhat in love with my father! She died in her nineties and asked me to be executor of her will, which was an honour and an example of our family friendship. The choir sang "All in the April evening" by Hugh S. Robertson at her funeral. I cried then, as I do now whenever I hear this. Below is a YouTube link to a performance.

https://youtu.be/Z8ojon1RJ4E?si=oW2sRZSwzoHJzTlt

My mother could not face attending my father's funeral and was upstairs at home when we and a few others returned. Mrs. Wheeldon went up. I overheard them talking. They were agreeing that it would be lovely if eventually Rosslynne and I got together.

Of course, we made friends in the choir. I am sorry, I cannot mention each of these. However, one is Connie Clamp. At one point, she was the patrons' secretary and put together the archive collection of the choir. She is 96 at the time of writing, and I visit her regularly in the care home where she now lives. Before that I visited her husband, Harry, who was in the same care home until his death, also in his nineties. They were Italophiles. Harry had fought in Italy in the Second World War and the family visited Italy almost every year for decades. He could speak Italian. We met them twice when we were staying at our house in Umbria.

Harry, Connie, me, Kath S, Kath O, and Alan at our house in Macchie, Umbria

Voluntary work after my retirement

I retired as a GP in 2005. Kath retired five years before me. She had established herself in various voluntary activities, including courses in art and winemaking. She died unexpectedly in February 2015. We did our separate things when it came to retirement activities, which was a refreshing change from when we worked as GP and practice manager together.

I have been a member of the Airedale Neighbourhood Management Board since just after its formation in 2008. It is a powerful community group which has done such a lot in the deprived area of Airedale and Ferry Fryston, Castleford. At the time of writing, I have been working with the amazing chair of the group, Mike Dixon. We are planning a fifteenth anniversary celebration event. It is amazing how many people have been involved with the group. Since I've been living alone, I have realised that meeting people, not necessarily just friends, is therapeutic for me. It is for most people. We organise a gala once a year, and I have a reputation of always arriving late to get out of lifting anything, such as tent poles, tables, etc. I absolutely love this photograph of my arrival at a gala, late as usual.

L to R, Mick Hutchinson, Steve Yates, Jo Parkin, and Mike Dixon

Mick is a retired coal miner. We went together on a lovely walk at the site where his coal mine used to be. He is a classic salt of the earth ex-miner who will do anything for anybody.

Steve died suddenly not many years ago. Kath and I got to know him on the relatively rare occasions when he was working for our council at an election. Part of his job was a scrutineer at our polling station. We always chatted with him when we voted. Jo has worked for Wakefield Council for many years and now has a senior position responsible for several communities in the Wakefield district. I have never forgotten the hug of friendship when I met her shortly after Kath's death. There was once a full-page article in our local paper with the headline "MR. AIREDALE". It was about Mike. He has been involved in so many things to do with our community. We often meet in a house as I am his vice chair.

I think there is a special friendship between people wanting to improve where they live. We are all in the same business. We can see the problems and strengths of our area. The relationship between people working for the community in a voluntary capacity is different from those contributing when they have paid jobs. It is not of any better quality. For me, there is a particular freedom when undertaking unpaid work.

Our local district councillors are associates of the board. There are three, and each does over and above what is expected of a councillor. I have written about Yvonne, who died, in Chapter 1. She was replaced by Jackie Ferguson, who is also a friendly person. A long-standing councillor is Les Shaw. Les and I meet regularly in my house, simply to have a coffee and chat together, mainly about the local political scene and more. He is a senior councillor and a member of the council cabinet. I have learned a lot from him. Kathryn Scott is the third who has been re-elected several times now. She helped me obtain my Irish passport by countersigning the documents several times when the process went wrong. I cannot find a photograph of all three councillors, but I cannot resist including this of a very happy Kathryn Scott dancing the maypole with Yvette Cooper, our MP, in the background. The other thing I admire about Kathryn is that she organises a regular litter pick. I decided that this is a form of social prescribing, which allows people to happily meet, work together, and do some good for the area by setting an example and showing the extent of the litter problem. When Kathryn dies, I have promised that I will fund a litter bin in Airedale dedicated to her name.

Cllr. Kathryn Scott

254

I became a trustee of Healthwatch Wakefield (HWW) in 2015 and was its chair for four years from 2016. As with my main career in general practice, I had a friendly relationship with the staff and I do regard the two CEOs with whom I have worked closely as friends. The first was Nichola Esmond, who was replaced by Gary Jevon. I hold them both in high esteem. I mentioned esteem to you as a quality of friendship at the very beginning of this chapter. They have told me they regard me as a friend. I last met them socially at the tenth anniversary of the birth of the charity. It was a big gathering of friends of the charity, as well as senior managers in the health and welfare community. When I was chair, I spent about an hour over a cuppa with each member of staff to get to know them better. I was astounded at their dedication. Even though not all of them are mentioned in this book, they know how highly I regarded them and still do. However, I must mention two more. Safeen Rehman is responsible for the volunteers, Young Healthwatch, and more. She introduced me to the organisation at the very start of my involvement. She is a very kind person and has always been very friendly and thoughtful towards me. We went to a national conference together to represent HWW and I got to know her better then. Sometimes, when I must speak, I get a laugh by saying, "I spent a couple of nights with Safeen in Nottingham." Helen Watkiss is the communications officer. She is very experienced and wise. She has been a great support to me. I have always felt I can ring her and have a chat about any problems. Indeed, some of us think she could have been the CEO.

Safeen Rehman, Healthwatch National Conference, Nottingham, 2017
Conference Dinner, Nottingham University

L to R: Helen Watkiss, Nichola Esmond, Gary Jevon, me.
Healthwatch National Conference, Stratford on Avon, 2018.
The Opposition Restaurant

The three friendship situations that follow have particular characteristics. The first two are new to me.

Befriending phone calls

I am a trustee in a small charity called Spectrum People. At the beginning of the pandemic in 2020, Tina Dransfield was employed to manage, amongst other things, the befriending service. I volunteered to telephone two people regularly. It did not work out for one. However, I have been telephoning a man (I will call him J) almost every Sunday afternoon for over three years. We speak for about 45 minutes. He lives on his own and has significant medical problems. He went to a private school and is middle class. He does not see many people. It took a while to establish rapport. We have never discussed the possibility of meeting. Our relationship is a friendly one and we can talk about anything. We discuss a lot of medical stuff regarding the NHS now. One of his medical problems is significant and it needs specialist attention. It is usually I who ends the conversation. After about a year and a half, in the middle of our conversation, he exclaimed loudly "Oh no!!" I asked him what had happened, and he replied, "They've scored." It was only then I realised he was watching football. He always has some form of sport on the television when we talk with the sound turned off. I think sport is his main interest. I feel this is a friendship where each of us can offload any worries on the other, and we respect one another's advice. I have a picture of his house in my mind. I can picture where he is sitting, a window and a door to the front garden and where the stairs are. He has not verbalised where these are, and they are created in my imagination. I have no picture in my mind of him, although I think he is short. It is not the same situation of two blind men who are friends. They would probably meet and shake hands, etc. It is not the same situation of two friends from different continents. More than likely, they would communicate using social media video methods on the internet. Jennifer Smith, mentioned above, for example, communicates with her sister in New Zealand like that and they talk together for hours. My friendship with J might be the same as before the internet, when the telephone was the only way of communicating at a distance. Did one ever phone up someone one never met? The Samaritans? Face-to-face, in person communication is the best for me. I am afraid I am not at all happy with spending time on the telephone with medical receptionists, advanced practitioners, general practitioners, and other medical people, which is what is happening now. It is a backward step and will cause a lot of trouble as time goes on.

Until recently, I had regular Saturday morning Zoom meetings with a friend, John Rouse. These is lasted two hours and we discussed all sorts, not just our personal experiences. Of course, these were important, especially when friends become ill or die. One interesting thing John did, after he heard I had written a chapter on social class, was to write a short piece himself about class. It ended up "What class do you think I am?" I told him I thought he was brought up working class, but now he lives a middle-class lifestyle. I have met John and his wife, Maggie. We were both trustees of a charity at one point. We stopped communicating by Zoom, because of the illness of one of John's relations and the illness of a friend.

A pen friend

In 2016, I went to a meeting of the St. Vincent DePaul Society congregation of my church. It was mentioned that there was a new research study managed by the English department of Leeds University. It was called "The Writing Project". An older person from outside of the university would be paired with a student on the English master's degree course. I volunteered. One of the rules was that one had to write by hand, which was interesting. I do have neat writing if I concentrate! Twice a year, there was a meeting between the students and the outside people. This was at the university for an afternoon of getting to know one another face-to-face over a cup of tea and a cake. My first student was towards the end of her course, so I got to know her only superficially.

In 2017 I was paired with a young woman called Sihan Qiao. She is also known as Hannah. She was charming and had a thirst for knowledge about our country. She taught me a lot about China.

I am sure we both enjoyed our communications. She has a good sense of humour. We continued communicating by email after she returned to Beijing at the end of her course. We exchange photographs and one I particularly remember is of the result of her cooking an English breakfast in Beijing. I will say no more than that it made me laugh. She is a good cook. She has a boyfriend and a good job. Her parents live quite a distance from Beijing in the country. If I were younger, I would visit Beijing.

Sihan Qiao (Hannah)

We communicate not as frequently as we did, but we always reply to one another's messages. It is a privilege for me to know somebody in Beijing.

Facebook

Part of the home page of my Facebook

In the last few days before writing this, I went out twice for lunch, each time with a couple. The first lunch was with friends and each of this couple were also Facebook friends of mine. The second couple I would describe as colleagues. When I mentioned Facebook, like many of my friends and people I know, they each told me they did not like Facebook. We did not discuss this further. I knew what their explanation would be.

Facebook label everyone who agree to share Facebook contents as "friends". Obviously, I do not have 390 people on my Facebook account homepage whom I regard as friends. Quite a few are ex-patients I have known for many years. Some are in the political world, like our local councillors. Some are my relations. Some are ex-colleagues. Some of these colleagues are very senior and at the top of their fields. Of people I regard as my friends, some live in Italy, Brazil, and the USA. Quite a few years ago, Richard Thornton asked if I would agree to be his Facebook friend. I had never heard of him. He lives in the USA. I did not immediately accept him as a Facebook friend but asked him why he wanted to link up. He explained that my mother was his mother's GP. My mother was involved in the delivery of baby Richard. His mother decided to call him after me! We did meet once when he came over to the UK.

A recent example of the power of and comfort given by Facebook was the sudden death of Tom, the son of my friend and ex-GP partner, Anne, at the age of 27 on 12 August 2023. Anne and her husband, Alan, announced the death on Facebook, and there were over 100 wonderful and compassionate return messages, which I am sure gave her, Alan, and her daughter, Sarah, great strength and support. Anne announced the funeral arrangements on Facebook.

I find Facebook is a fantastic comfort, particularly since Kath died. She was also an active Facebook user. I look at my Facebook pages every morning. I don't like foul language on Facebook and put any such messages into the background. I have been hacked a couple of times, but that does not put me off.

I am also signed on to LinkedIn, WhatsApp, and Twitter.

Late friends

Orders of service from some of the funerals I have attended

I have mentioned one or two deaths of friends in this chapter. The photograph above is of some shelves in my study. I will only mention one person who died, because thinking of him and his death always makes me smile. He made me smile when he was alive. His name is Bill Clift. He did some fantastic voluntary work for Castleford and the constituency Labour Party. I first met him in a Chinese takeaway on Wheldon Road, Castleford, in the middle of some elections when I was standing for the Social Democratic Party. He was campaigning for the Labour Party. Although we were political enemies, he was very friendly and amusing as we talked while we waited for our takeaways. I came across him many times over the years, and one of those meetings was unexpected. I was fortunate to be selected for a ticket to a spectacular service at St Paul's Cathedral, London. It was only open to those who had had an award from the Most Excellent Order of the British Empire. Bill and I had each been awarded an MBE, him before me. I did not realise he was going to this service and noticed him as I was looking for a seat. We sat together.

Bill Clift on my left at St Paul's Cathedral

The service was spectacular because of the presence of the Queen and Prince Philip (who was the Grand Master of the Order), trumpeters, an orchestra with choir, and all the bells chiming at one point.

Why does my thinking of Bill's death make me smile? One of his many voluntary jobs was to be a lay member of inspection teams which checked on general practice targets. The teams met together once a year at the offices of the Primary Care Trust. Bill was 20 minutes late for one of these meetings. He came into the meeting room and announced, "Good afternoon. I am the late Bill Clift." He really is now.

In this chapter and throughout the rest of the book, I have not included all my friends. To those I haven't mentioned, I give you my apologies once again, and hope you understand. Each friendship has been instrumental in making me the person I have become, and I am truly grateful. Thank you.

Index of People

Milton Keynes UK
Ingram Content Group UK Ltd.
UKHW021046080524
442352UK00001B/39